Windfall of Inherited Treasures

Windfall of Inherited Treasures

WITH WATERCOLOR ILLUSTRATIONS
BY BETTY CARNEY TAUSSIG

Windfall Publishing Company, Inc., P.O. Box 469, Annapolis, Maryland 21404

To Beloved Anna Lee
who has honored me with so beautiful a treasure.
May I live up to the trust she has placed in me.

And To Joe
my husband, who is not my severest critic, who has provided me with the time
and space to record this small colorful spot in American History, and whose hands are
always open and ready to applaud whatever I do.

And For
our son, Joe, our daughter, Susan, and our grandchildren, Vail, Chris, and Matthew.

"SUNNYSIDE"—1844
Aquasco, Maryland

Built by my great-great-grandfather, Dr. Michael Jenifer Stone, for his bride, Susan Ann Somervell, the hyphen and the house were added on to an 18th Century outdoor kitchen.

"Michael Stone House" — B. Taussig '81
Aquasco - Md.

ACKNOWLEDGEMENTS

I would like to acknowledge and thank my late aunt, Anna Lee Turner, and my mother, Grace Craycroft Carney, for sharing our family history and lore with me. Others, without whom this story would never have been written, are the late Betty Briscoe of the Calvert County Historical Society whose vast store of county history filled in the gaps in records burned by the Puritans and a court house fire and, for their constant generosity with their time and resources, Mr. Charles Perrygo of the Charles County Historical Society, Eunice Turner of Aquasco whose own recollections of village lore and collection of memorabilia shed more light on Woodville history, Nancy Helmly whose ancestors came from the plantation adjoining Bishop Claggett's home, Mr. James Patton of "Gaymont", Port Royal, Virginia, who trusted me with a cherished family book with letters from General Lafayette and Scottish relatives to the Somerville family, Mrs. Barbara Willis of the Rappahannock Library in Fredericksburg, Virginia, and Judge Francis Waller of the Spotsylvania, Virginia, museum, Mr. Peter Mallett of the Georgia Vermont Historical Society, Mr. Edmund Steele of the St. Albans' Historical Society and Mr. Edwin Beitzell of St. Mary's County, author of many books on that most historical county, also, Mr. George King, a foremost genealogist of Fredericksburg, Virginia, who made the Saunders-Sanders connection for me, Commander J. More-Nisbett of Edinburgh, son of the well-known Scottish genealogist, and James Hall who filled in many pieces of the John Wilkes Booth story.

Also the late Arthur Neumann, a foremost genealogist of Maryland, who supplied me with many facts and fascinating tidbits of Maryland History.

And John Scofield, an old friend who read my first draft and told me "like it was."

FOREWORD

Some years ago, a friend of mine inherited an 18th Century desk which had always been in her family. Her mother had neglected to tell her of its history and this so distressed her that I realized that this could happen to me. So I set out to learn of my ancestors and our family possessions. This led to a great adventure that I put in booklet form for my children. Eventually the booklet was requested by three historical societies and I had the added fun of helping a man make a connection he had been seeking for 30 years.

After I inherited "Sunnyside" or the "Michael Stone House" as it is registered as an historic site by Prince George's County, and had sifted every corner and every inch as carefully as an archeologist for more than two years, it seemed almost inevitable that the next step was to tell an amazing story of one family as it lived American History, for the treasures I found in the attic revealed new lights on major phases of history.

"Sunnyside" had been built by my great-great-grandfather, Dr. Michael Jenifer Stone, for his bride, Susan Ann Somervell, in 1844. The house was connected by a hyphen to an 18th Century outdoor kitchen containing a large fireplace dating it probably prior to 1740.

The unraveling of the stories of these two people and the remarkable families from which they came was to unfold history from the beginning of Maryland through their own times.

I cannot help but feel that the story of Susan Somervell's family—the Somerville family is the same as the story of the Scottish ancestors of thousands of Americans if their ancestors came in the 17th or 18th Centuries prior to 1745, for England and Scotland were at odds and it is probable that all Scots in the English colonies came as prisoners and were of noble birth.

So much of this history has been lost, for the British destroyed castles, houses, and above all records during the Jacobite wars and even changed family names when prisoners were sent to the colonies as indentured servants. And here in America the history has been lost after nine generations. What fiber lies in these marvelous Scots who have given us over 50 percent of our presidents, so out of proportion from the tiny Scottish population to our own huge one.

As I sifted through treasures accumulated for generations perhaps no discovery was so shocking as ferreting our family secrets of the Civil War. It is my hope that in the telling of the tale I can shed a new light on the main players of a tragic page in our history, for I feel a new-to-me admiration, honor, and affection for President Lincoln, coming as I do from a family that has taught each new generation to hate this poor man. I feel a deep compassion for Mrs. Lincoln to whom history has been most unkind. A woman from a southern family who lost three brothers fighting for the Confederacy, her own deep convictions must have made her position unendurable and when at last the conflict was to cost the life of her husband whom she did love dearly, it is small wonder that she lost her mind.

And John Wilkes Booth, perhaps I paint a somewhat different picture than history records. His name has lived in infamy, with all but many Southerners who dared not say out loud what they really felt, all but a few brave souls like Oden Bowie, elected Governor of Maryland four years after the Civil War, who named his son George Washington Booth Bowie. And Frederick Stone, a judge and future U.S.

congressman who courageously was counsel for the young David Herold, who accompanied Booth on his flight and was later hanged.

Booth during the Civil War had smuggled medical supplies to the South. His sister, Asia, wrote a book published years later by her granddaughter telling of his role as a smuggler of medical supplies particularly desperately needed quinine water.

His spectacular act just several days after Lee's surrender was in his mind an act of war for Lee's other generals had not yet surrendered. He believed he was saving his much-loved South, that he would go south to join the generals who had still not surrendered, the war would continue, and the South would win. Knowing full well his act might cost his life his main concern was what he was bringing on his family, particularly his mother.

When I had read much of this man I could not help but feel a certain sympathy for him for my own father, as Chief of Staff to Admiral Halsey in World War II was on the war criminals list of the enemy and had we lost the war would have been executed. Perhaps heroes and villains in war are only winners and losers.

How little did I know as I began the laborious task of sorting family boxes in the attic that many members of my family were to play participating roles in the dime-novel activities of the last year of the Civil War.

And so what this book is all about is a peephole of American History as revealed through the family of my great-great-grandparents, and the treasures I found in their house, telling tales of history you might never find in your history book.

CONTENTS

LIST OF ILLUSTRATIONS

DR. MICHAEL JENIFER STONE
and his wife
SUSAN ANN SOMERVELL

About whom, with their families, this tale revolves.

SOUTHERN MARYLAND

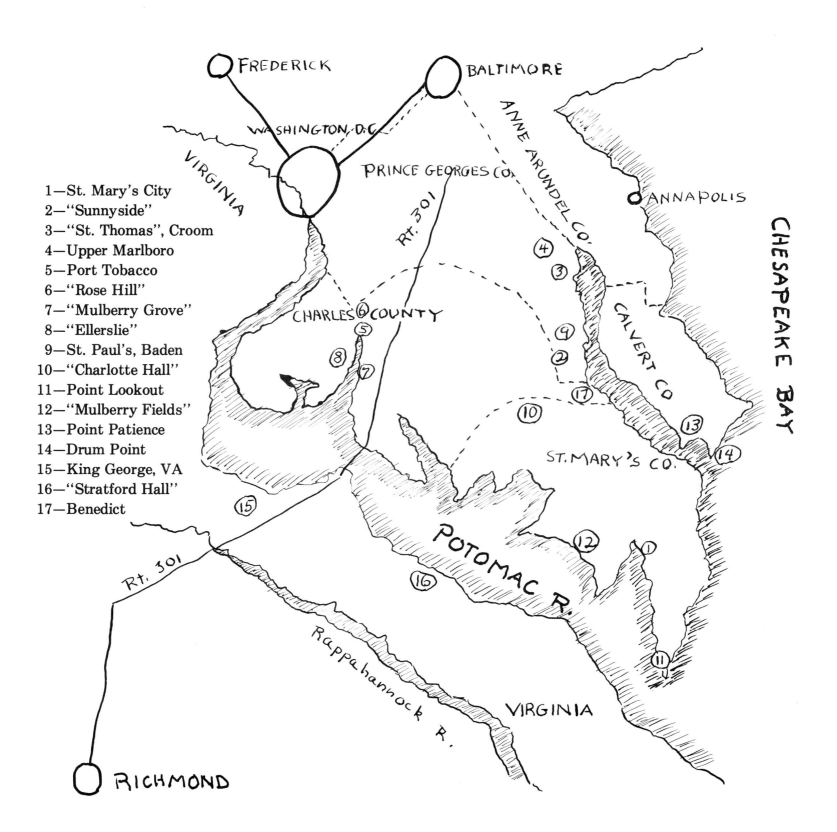

1—St. Mary's City
2—"Sunnyside"
3—"St. Thomas", Croom
4—Upper Marlboro
5—Port Tobacco
6—"Rose Hill"
7—"Mulberry Grove"
8—"Ellerslie"
9—St. Paul's, Baden
10—"Charlotte Hall"
11—Point Lookout
12—"Mulberry Fields"
13—Point Patience
14—Drum Point
15—King George, VA
16—"Stratford Hall"
17—Benedict

CHAPTER I   OF INDIANS AND EARLY SETTLERS

As Joe and I turned from the grave side at St. Mary's Chapel, we looked across the field at the house in the distance. Childhood memories returned in a flood. The village around us was wet from a spring rain and the almost imperceptible hue of pale green and rose spread over the landscape. There was a stirring and awakening of the world from a long winter's sleep.

The white house glistened in the sun against the disappearing dark cloud of the rain, strong and unpretentious it seemed eternal, like a beacon filled with the spirits of the brave and the creators of the highest quality of life, a model to look to and go forward with, to learn from and take to the future.

How strange and detached I felt from this house where I had never spent so much as a night in this house that had been built by my great-great-grandfather but where as I sifted through the accumulation of centuries so carefully and comprehensively of the possessions of my ancestors I experienced the sensation of living each step of American History myself—as if I were there—as if it were actually happening to me.

My mother had been raised in this house and all of her ancestors for three hundred and fifty years had come from Southern Maryland, but she had married in the Navy and my life had been a traveling one. Summers, Christmases, and Thanksgivings had sometimes been spent with my grandfather on the adjoining farm and as we walked across the field happy memories flowed in a rambling rush, visions of roaring fireplaces in every room and laughter, quiet moments in the library with "The Bobbsie Twins," charging through the house in dirty old lion skins from my grandfather's African game trophies, blackberry picking, catching minnows in the streams with friends, and wonderful village picnics at Benedict with tables and tables of dream-world food from ancient Maryland recipes. And the wonderful village people so skilled in the art of beautiful daily living and still maintaining the best traditions of their English and Scottish ancestors.

Finally we came to the house and we laughed as if Anne Lee, my mother's sister, were with us for she had locked the door but had left the downstairs windows open in case she had forgotten her key.

But inside she seemed to be everywhere and I understand why it was so difficult for her devoted sisters-in-law to go inside after that day.

Anna Lee was my mother's much younger sister. Fun-loving and gregarious she had no children but still I was surprised that she had willed me the house and farm. While I knew she would leave me family heirlooms it was still unexpected until I came to realize that she had viewed herself as not the owner of this treasure but rather as a custodian from generation to generation. She had passed a trust to me and so it was that for the next two and one half years I went through the house inch by inch, sifting and evaluating and making certain that unusual artifacts of intrinsic value would be insured of enduring preservation by being in the right museum. It was hard work both physically and mentally, requiring much research, but always I knew I had been given an incredible gift and from the beginning I knew this was to be a joyous and extraordinary adventure.

My husband Joe and I entered the house and as he had been named executor of her will he sat down at the lovely old 18th century desk and began to sort papers. Soon he stumbled upon a box with a small gold pin in the shape of a scroll. It was inscribed "Palmum qui Meruit Ferat", with the initials W.S. and the date, February 22, 1797. This was the first treasure and the beginning of a wonderful reliving of American History, as curious items began to pop up here and there in the old house. Calling a catholic priest I asked for a translation for I am Episcopalian and as I told him, an Episcopalian is a Catholic who flunked Latin. He kindly translated, "He who deserves the power or the glory will carry it away." Later I was to find that this was the motto of Charlotte Hall the first military preparatory school in the United States, and the pin was given as a prize in debating contests. Family research shows it was given to Dr. Stone's brother William Stone.

The house had been built in 1844 by my great-great-grandparents on a 1698 family land grant to another branch of the family. Known then as the village of Woodville (and still called that by the oldtimers) the present day post office is Aquasco, named for the Indian tribe of that area. During the 18th Century it was known as a very elegant community. The houses were spacious, the ladies fashionable and the appointments of daily life were carried out in the tradition of their cavalier ancestors.

The house was built onto an 18th Century outside kitchen for apparently there had been an 18th Century house there before. Today an 18th Century corn crib and a meat house also remain to attest to a previous house.

Dr. Michael Jenifer Stone and his wife, Susan Ann Somervell, both came from fascinating families and researching both heritages took me through every important phase of American History in a vivid way.

Dr. Stone's great-great-great-grandfather, William Stone, was the first Protestant Governor of Maryland. Captured by the Puritans at Annapolis during the Cromwellian period when Charles, the First, had his head chopped off, he was imprisoned for three years. A great-grandmother was a sister of John Hanson, the first President of the United States, and his own father was elected to Congress the same year that George Washington became President.

Susan Somervell Stone's great-great-grandfather was the twelfth Lord Somerville of Scotland. Captured by the English in the 1715 Jacobite uprising, the Hall of Records in Annapolis shows he came into Annapolis in chains on the "Godspeed." The ship's manifest also shows two other Scots of noble birth, James Magruder, and a MacPherson, who became large plantation owners near Woodville.

I have long been fascinated with the Scots amongst us. Woodville is full of Scottish names all considered to be "well-born." Sir Walter Scott says in his "Tales of a Grandfather," that in the 1715 uprising only the educated and the leaders were exiled to the colonies for the colonies needed these men to help develop the new land. The rest of the prisoners were hanged.

Captured Scots were sent to the colonies during three periods, 1649 for resisting Cromwell, in 1715 in an attempt to put the son of James, the Second, back on the English throne, and in 1745 for the uprising led by "Bonnie Prince Charlie" on behalf of his father. Not many survived the latter rebellion.

Ninian Beall was a prisoner of the 1649 rebellion. Sold into indenture in Southern Maryland, he soon acquired himself so many land grants his nervous English mentors had to clamp down on him. There was a saying in the colonies, "Watch out for the Scots!" Ninian Beall was buried at Dumbarton Oaks in Washington, D.C. and recently when they had to move his grave to build a road they found his was six feet seven and had flaming red hair!

There is some evidence that once the Scots were in the colonies and no longer a threat, the English set them up according to their stations in life, for James Somervell showed up in Calvert County two years after his arrival (not having completed his seven years' indenture) owning large tracts of land at the mouth of the Patuxent River and eventually he became the High Sheriff of Calvert County.

On a table in the living room was a metal box filled with arrowheads that had been collected from the farm when the rains had washed the loose dirt from the newly plowed fields to leave them exposed. Running my fingers through them I could not help but think of the Indians of Southern Maryland, so gentle, so civilized and so helpful to the early settlers.

When the first settlers came on the Ark and the Dove in 1634, they found peace-loving Indians living in oblong houses in villages, and growing gardens. The only warring they did was to defend their territory from the raiding Susquahannocks, for their land was so bountiful with fish, oysters, geese, ducks, deer and even an occasional buffalo that they had no need to compete for survival.

The Indians of St. Mary's County gave half of their gardens to the first settlers for they arrived too late to plant. Lord Calvert protected them against raiding Indians and forbid the settling anywhere within three miles of an Indian village. The daughter of the King of the Piscataways, at his request was adopted by Margaret Brent, educated in England, and later married Giles Brent, the brother-in-law of Lord Calvert.

Toward the end of the 17th Century while Lord Calvert was away in England, brutal Indian raids occurred across the Potomac in Virginia. Governor Berkeley of Virginia, who at four years old had seen his mother and father murdered and scalped by Indians blamed the Maryland Piscataways for these raids. At his insistance Colonel Truman, head of the Maryland militia, joined the Virginia Captain at the Piscataway village where ten hostages were taken until the dispute could be settled. But at the order of the Virginia Captain the hostages were shot. Mysteriously and over night the Indians disappeared never to be heard of again. Some believe they went to Ohio.

Lord Calvert on his return from England was furious and disciplined Colonel Truman for his role in the tragic event. In view of the history of Maryland Indians it is probable that the raid was by Susquahannocks. The only remaining evidence of our Indians today is a people who call themselves "we sorts", a mixture of slaves, Indians, and white people. "We sorts" are still to be found in Woodville.

I gave my box of arrowheads along with old tools, locks, and kitchen utensils to a small state museum at Clinton, Maryland. One arrowhead was determined to have come from upstate New York where the rare rock exists in only one county in the world.

And so the first settlers came to Maryland in 1634 clearing the land and building fine homes at the mouth of the Potomac and soon after at the mouth of the Patuxent.

George Calvert, a close friend of King James I was Catholic and because of the severe persecution of Catholics at that time in England the king created the Irish barony of Baltimore giving him the status of baron in England, but the rank of earl in Maryland. He had granted Lord Calvert a proprietership at first in Newfoundland, for as Newfoundland is on the same parallel with England it was thought to have the same climate. Lord Calvert took his colony to this harsh land and by the end of the first year many had perished. The king then granted him a land more favorable in climate "like Virginia", but Lord Calvert died the following year after his return from Newfoundland, the grim experience probably having broken his health. His son, Cecelius, became the second Lord Baltimore.

Cecelius' brother, Leonard Calvert, came as governor with both Catholics seeking religious freedom, and Episcopalians, for Maryland was founded with religious freedom for all, unlike Virginia where only Episcopalians could colonize. Soon this was to be the undoing of Maryland when trouble-making Puritans were invited to leave Virginia and were kindly invited to live in Maryland where they founded Annapolis. They repaid the kindness of Lord Calvert by overthrowing his government with the help and support of Lord Cromwell's ships standing off of Annapolis.

Maryland was unique in its founding in that land was granted only to those who could afford to pay the passage of 20 indentured servants. Thus they came like many small companies that were sufficient unto themselves and for nearly a hundred years there were virtually no towns in Maryland. There were perhaps a thousand land grants the first hundred years, but there was a curious aspect of this. If a younger son of an English nobleman were successful in his venture he could apply to the College of Arms in London and receive the status of baron in Maryland carrying the same coat of arms with crest as his ancestors. Ordinarily this right would belong only to the oldest son. There were one hundred and eleven baronies established in Maryland the first hundred years, until slavery was to change the plantation system.

Many grants were given to descendants of those who had given meritorious service to the crown such as a large early grant to the Ashcom family on the lower Patuxent, for he was a descendant of the Ashcom who was the beloved tutor to Queen Elizabeth, the First.

With Lord Calvert came Father Andrew White and his Jesuit priests and Cecelius Calvert, Second Lord Baltimore, cautioned the new Catholic colonists that, "all acts of Roman Catholique Religion to be done as privately as may be and that they instruct all Roman Catholiques to be silent upon all occasions of discourse concerning matters of religion and that the said Governor and commissioners treat Protestants with as much mildness and favor as Justice will permit. This in order that no complaint be made in Virginia or England." And so it was that few Catholic churches were established but rather chapels were built on the plantations. But also fear of the power of any church resulted in few Episcopal churches of substance until the early 18th Century when Queen Anne, a staunch Episcopalian, decreed that an Episcopal church be built every ten miles in Maryland. Because of this, Maryland has many lovely 18th Century Episcopal churches but few Catholic churches or even chapels of the early days remain.

Further up the Patuxent, Thomas Hollyday, an ancestor of Susan Somervell was granted a large tract of land. The Hollydays were a fascinating family. Not listed as being of the Scottish nobility, nevertheless, Leonard Hollyday was knighted by James the First of England in 1605 and was made Lord Mayor of London. Understandably the Hollydays were persona non grata in Scotland for they were marauders in the Lowlands. The night before terrorizing the countryside they would go up on a high hill and debauch until dawn, and the fearful people called them the "Holidays." When Richard, the First, of England called for five thousand men for an army, one thousand were Hollydays.

Thomas Hollyday applied to the College of Arms in London and was granted the same coat of arms as Leonard, the Lord Mayor of London. Leonard Hollyday was a great favorite of Queen Elizabeth, the First, and when the great pageant was held in her honor in 1602 his contribution to the celebration was fifty thousand pounds. "Billingsley Point" built by Thomas Hollyday in 1680, is one of the oldest houses in Maryland.

Although in England the inheritance of baronies went only to the oldest son, it would appear that younger sons who established themselves successfully in Maryland could apply and receive the status of baron using their family coat of arms and sometimes retaining the phonetics of the family name while changing the spelling.

Susan Somervell's mother was a Hollyday.

Those who received baronies could be either Baron Court Leet, Court Baron, or both. Baron Court Baron meant that he was authorized to administer the affairs of the Lord Proprietor such as collecting taxes, for the taxes were paid to the Lord Proprietor instead of the king although the king required a symbolic tax of two arrowheads a year. Baron Court Leet gave the authority to administer punishment.

The houses were built with a large center hall where court or administrative business was held.

Soon after the settling came more worshippers seeking religious freedom—the French Huguenots. Their names tell us that they too were predominately of the French aristocracy—leaders who would add a dimension of beauty and culture to Southern Maryland. After a hundred years of exile in England, these French Huguenots had brought with them their highly developed culture having taught the English weaving in silk, and more refined goldsmithing and architecture. The nobility of some of these Frenchmen is indicated by the crown on the crest of their coat of arms and many Southern Marylanders of French descent show the crown on their family crests.

William Stone had arrived in the new world in 1633, the year before the coming of the Ark and the Dove. Settling on the lower Eastern Shore at Hungars Creek, his company consisted of thirty-three indentured servants, an East Indian and a Turkish bodyguard.

King Charles was concerned by the development of the Eastern Shore by the Dutch and the Swedes and was encouraging more English settling even sending part of the Jamestown colony to this end.

Just before the last decade of the sixteen hundreds, William and Mary came to the throne of England as firm Episcopalians. The Episcopalians and Protestants now outnumbered Catholics by twenty-five to

"ST. THOMAS"—1769
Croom, Maryland

Built in 1769 as a Chapel of Ease to "St. Paul's" of Baden, many of the noble family of Calverts are buried beneath the floor boards including Eleanor Calvert, wife of John Park Custis, George Washington's stepson. She was the mother of the builder of Woodlawn in Virginia and the grandmother of the builder of Arlington.

Bishop Claggett, the first Episcopal bishop consecrated in the United States, and his wife were originally buried beneath the floor under a slab inscribed in Latin written by Francis Scott Key. Later they were disinterred and are now buried at the Washington Cathedral.

This was the parish of Daniel of St. Thomas Jenifer, signer of the Constitution, and slave agent of Kunta Kinte of "Roots."

The British passed this church on their way to and from Washington in 1814.

Many of Susan Somervell's Hollyday relatives are buried here for her mother was a Hollyday.

B. Taussig '82

one in Maryland and they took the opportunity of the support of the new regime to overthrow the government of the Lord Proprietor in a fairly bloodless coup. At the same time, the holding of public office by a Catholic was outlawed—a law which held until the Revolution.

The reign of William and Mary was brief but during this period Maryland was laid out in Episcopal parishes and a college, King William College was begun in Annapolis that still exists as St. John's College today.

During a brief reign by Queen Anne it was decreed that an Episcopal church be built every ten miles and she gave the communion silver to each of these churches. Many churches were rebuilt toward the end of the 18th Century but still retain the cherished Queen Anne silver. For the next twenty-five years Maryland was governed by a Royal Governor until 1715 at which time Benedict Calvert petitioned King George, the First, to have the proprietorship restored. At an early age he had learned that the privileges of his family would never be restored as long as he remained a Roman Catholic and even before the death of his father he had converted to the Church of England. And so, the Proprietorship of Maryland was returned to the Calvert family until the Revolution.

CHAPTER II   THOSE INCREDIBLE SCOTS

It was this same year, 1715, that brought a large number of Scottish prisoners to the colonies. Known as Jacobites they had participated in the Rebellion against England to place the son of James, the Second, on the throne. According to Fitzroy McLean, "In a Concise History of Scotland" those of noble birth had their titles removed, their estates were destroyed, and their names changed. Sir Walter Scott says in his "Tales of a Grandfather" that the prisoners, most of them "of birth and education" were taken to Newgate, Marshalsea, and other prisons of London. At the same time their families were taken to London, but were left with apparent freedom to come and go.

Then an extraordinary thing happened. Because of the station in life of the prisoners the prisons became a party place for the socialites of London. Sir Walter Scott says "the prisons overflowed with wine and good cheer . . . money, it is said, circulated so plentifully among them, that when it was difficult to obtain silver for a guinea in the streets, nothing was so easy to find change whether of gold or of silver, in the jail. A handsome young Highland gentleman made such an impression on the fair visitors who came to minister to the wants of the captured that some reputations were put in peril by the excess of their attentions to this favorite object of compassion."

But when the many bills of high treason were charged against them, thoughts turned from frivolity to escape. Some did escape, even one earl by the wits of his ingenious wife, escaped from the Tower of London.

But James Somervell, great-great-grandfather of Susan Somervell was not so fortunate.

His name having been changed from Somerville to Somervell, James, the twelfth Lord Somerville of Scotland appears on the ship's manifest of the "Godspeed." This document in the Hall of Records in Annapolis also shows he had been incarcerated at Newgate. And so he came into Annapolis in chains where the record shows he was purchased by Dr. Gustavus Brown, the Elder, of "Rich Hill" also a Scot who had been exiled himself seven years before in another Jacobite uprising. There is some evidence that they may have been related. "Rich Hill" was to play a key role in Booth's escape during the Civil War.

It is probable that these Scottish leaders, so necessary to help develop the colonies were actually financed by the English once they were no longer a threat to England, for two years later James Somervell made a large land purchase at the mouth of the Patuxent River and the 1733 Rent Rolls show him with 12 slaves, a large number for that period.

James Somervell, as he was now called, was 41 years old at the time of his capture. Back in Scotland he left 8 children at least two of whom were sons. James, the older, was seventeen at the time. He also left a wife, Janet, who our family lore says, died of a broken heart. James, the son, was given three hundred pounds a year by the English for himself and his brothers and sisters. A portrait of him at the "Drum," the family house near Edinburgh, shows him in a red coat with a mass of flowing white curls.

James, the son, had been raised in London following the 1715 Rebellion according to his station in life. Thirteen years later he returned to Scotland having been granted "the permission of Glasgow to enter Scotland" with a very rich English wife, having denied the Jacobite cause and having given his allegiance to the Hanovers. Scottish records also show he was the twelfth Lord Somerville of Scotland since the English did not recognize his father's existence.

Then began the most beautiful restoration of "Drum House," the family house in Gilmerton outside of Edinburgh, by the Architect William Adam, the father of the famous Adam brothers. Enclosed in the house are two Norman rooms, probably all that remained after the house was destroyed in 1715. Also destroyed was the family castle "Cowthally" in Lanark, one of the 80 Norman castles built following the Norman invasion. James, "The Restorer", placed the large stone coat of arms from "Cowthally" in the garden wall of "Drum House." Over the stairs, the breath-taking ceiling is carved with birds, flowers, and fruit and at the head of the stairs are the heads of three leopards, two and one, the leopards having been carried by William the Conqueror and having been the armorial bearing of the Somervilles prior to the Holy Wars.

In 1756 the Mercat (Market) Cross of Edinburgh was removed to "Drum House," a terrible reminder that Jacobites and the losers in the wars were hanged here. In place of the unicorn with vane, it was surmounted with the cross crosslet undoubtedly having some significance with the cross crosslet of the Fitche of the Somerville arms. Before this cross public proclamations were read and criminals were hanged.

The original cross was restored to its original place in Edinburgh in 1866 and a duplicate was placed in its stead at the "Drum" where it remains today. Before the original cross, "Bonnie Prince Charlie" proclaimed his father King James the VIII of Scotland during his brief occupancy of Edinburgh.

In 1745 stragglers from "Bonnie Prince Charlie's" army were seen approaching "Drum House." The family threw the silver out the window into the tall grass, hid the family jewels in a tree trunk and themselves in cupboards in the attic. Still five Highlanders and three villagers were killed in this encounter. Later "Bonnie Prince Charlie" apologized no doubt knowing of the tragedy the Jacobite allegiance had already caused this family.

Although it is certain the twelfth Lord Somerville never returned to Scotland letters in the possession of the Tiernan family indicate his second American born son, James, made many trips to Scotland as an agent for himself and his older brother John who always used the Somerville spelling. And there is evidence that at least two of his American born daughters married and lived in Scotland for one letter from Lady Gordon to James Somervell pleads for financial help for one destitute sister and her children and another letter to John from a brother-in-law in Scotland thanks him for financial help. For "King Tobacco" had soon made the latest Scottish immigrants extremely prosperous, more so than even when they were Scottish barons.

At the same time James Somerville was captured, George Wemyss, third son of the Earl of Wemyss was killed and his widow, Betty, came to Annapolis with her three small children, their names having been changed to Weems. Her oldest son James settled on the Patuxent River and was the ancestor of many illustrious Americans. He married Margaret Terrett from Westmoreland County, Virginia, who had a brother, Washington Terrett. It is probable the Terretts were related to the Washington family. His nephew the famous "Parson" Weems wrote, "The Life and Memorable Actions of George Washington" which tells the famous George Washington and the Cherry Tree story. "Parson" Weems had studied doctoring with his uncle and no doubt enjoyed many visits with his cousins and the Washington family. It was to the Wemyss family that the famous MacDuff who slew MacBeth belonged.

The Jacobite exiles stayed close together for the Weems family married into the Somervell family and in the third generation the Magruders and Somervells were to marry.

It is a curious thing that although the spelling of the names of the Scottish noblemen were changed there is some evidence that some of the oldest sons took back the original Scottish spelling. Some Magruders appear as McGregors in family bibles and James' oldest son John used the Somerville spelling.

After two years with Dr. Gustavas Brown, the Elder, James Somervell purchased Point Patience, near Solomons Island with a house built by Ashcom in the 17th Century, four rooms of which are still standing and enclosed in the Commanding Officer's Quarters at the Naval Weapons Station. Solomons Island was probably part of this purchase for at one time it was known as Somervell Island. In all probability he later built a house a little further down at "Drum" Point for the coincidence of the name is too great—"Drum" being Gaelic for "the backside of the hill." He became a doctor and three years later married Sarah Howe whose grandparents were both Puritans and French Huguenots.

Sarah and Dr. James had three sons, John, James, and Alexander. In 1748 Dr. James built the beautiful Middleham Chapel a few miles north of Point Patience and his son Alexander rebuilt the lovely Christ Church in 1769 at Prince Frederick still standing to remind us of those irrepressible, productive Scots.

In the middle of the 18th Century, Southern Maryland flourished elegantly. George Mason's brother from Port Tobacco had brought an indentured servant, William Buckland to Charles County. After building many public buildings he turned his hand to the building of many Annapolis and Southern Maryland homes. His graceful almost French hand in architecture had, by the middle of the 18th Century earned Annapolis the reputation of "the Paris of British America."

When "Bonnie Prince Charlie" arrived in Scotland in 1745 many of the Scottish noblemen whose clans had participated in the 1715 uprising had pledged their loyalty to the Hanovers and their baronies, earldoms, and estates had been returned to them. But "Bonnie Prince Charlie" with only a handful of followers so captured the hearts and imagination of the Scots that as he swept across Scotland to Edinburgh, many of the clans who still in their hearts believed the descendants of their own Mary Queen of Scots to be the rightful heirs to the throne abandoned their Hanovarian allegiance and joined forces in the Jacobite cause again. Such loyalists were the Murrays, (James Somervell's first wife was a Murray) and the MacPhersons. It is said that even as late as 1777 when "Bonnie Prince Charlie" was exiled in Italy the MacPhersons sent him a message that they were ready "to go again."

In the village of Woodville there is a Scottish family by the name of Forbes. Considered to be well-born they nevertheless have lost the records of how they came to Southern Maryland, and so have the MacPhersons. In the 1745 uprising the Forbes and the Somervilles maintained their oaths to the English Hanovers.

Although prisoners were sent to the plantations in 1745 most did not fare too well, for the English were determined that this would be the last uprising. The wounded were killed on the battle fields, the wearing of the kilt or the plaids were forbidden and even the playing of the bagpipes was verboten.

In 1755 during the French and Indian Wars General Braddock from his headquarters at Frederick, Maryland, set out to capture Fort Duquesne (now Pittsburgh). The British troops unfamiliar with the fighting ways of Indians found themselves trapped and ambushed.

Colonel George Washington took command and led the British troops to safety, under the cover of darkness retreating to Philadelphia. In 1758 a force of 5,000 militia men and twelve hundred Scottish Highlanders under the Command of General Forbes finally took Fort Duquesne. The fierce commando-like tactics of Highlanders on the battlefield were well-known and used to advantage.

John Somerville, the oldest American-born son of Lord Somervell, built the beautiful "Mulberry Fields" in the mid 18th Century on the Potomac having married the daughter of another Jacobite exile. High on a hill with a sweeping view to the Potomac a mile away, "Mulberry Fields" was so named for a not too successful venture of growing silk worms. Beautifully kept by the present owners with lovely gardens, one can still see the old weaving house, summer kitchen, and carriage house. A cannonball that didn't quite make it from a British warship in the War of 1812 sits on the back porch. Letters in the possession of the Tiernan family indicate a large number of slaves escaped to a British ship below and the British captain refused to return them against their will.

One son of John's, George Somerville, was a surgeon in the Revolution. A bachelor, his charming house is now quarters at the Patuxent Naval Base. When George died he left his estate to his brothers providing they would free his slaves.

John's grandson, William C. Somerville, was a most fascinating man. A fun-loving bachelor he purchased "Stratford Hall," the birthplace of Robert E. Lee, in 1818 in order to be near the bright lights and the more festive social life of Richmond.

In 1825 John Quincy Adams appointed him minister to Sweden. (President Adams wife, Louisa Johnson, was a Southern Maryland girl from Calvert County, her father having been the first governor of Maryland after the Revolution.)

In this same year General Lafayette came to the United States to celebrate the 50th Anniversary of the Revolution. Perhaps his great role in the American Revolution was to save his life in the French Revolution for the rabble of Paris was without mercy for the noblemen of France, but although the Marquise de Lafayette did not loose his head to the guillotine he was imprisoned for five years. His wife, who elected to be imprisoned with him, became ill and died in prison.

General Lafayette renewed his friendships in the United States visiting the Madison family, and other close friends before returning to Europe on the same ship with William Somerville, his close friend, who was on his way to Sweden.

On the voyage William Somerville became mortally ill, and at his request was buried at "La Grange", the estate of General Lafayette in France.

The following is a letter to William's brother Henry from General Lafayette.

"La Grange", January 20, 1826

My Dear Sir:

"It is to me a very painful, but sacred duty to be among the first to convey the dire information of your having lost an excellent Brother, and I, a most valued friend, who on the last moment has honored me with an additional and most precious mark of his affection.

"You know that during our passage, and since our arrival in France, the health of Mr. Somerville has been declining.

"However anxious he was, to fulfill his Honorable Mission, he found himself forcibly detained in Paris; nor could he even meet our invitation to await better times in the bosom of our Family, and when his physician yielded to his opportunities to let him proceed to the South, every Hope to save him had been given up.

"An account of the lamentable event will be transmitted by the proper authorities. I shall confine myself to his expressed intention to entrust us at La Grange, with the care of his mortal remains. The affecting wish had been in a recent interview, mentioned with a most friendly earnestness, and was repeated to Dr. Lucas on the very day of his death.

"Amidst the deep feelings of affection, no time was lost, and while my son remained here to watch over the precious charge, I hastened to consult with the Minister and other officers of the United States in Paris, on the method by which duty, respect and affection towards him might best be gratified—their joint opinion being that the Cemetery where two of my grandchildren are deposited, was the proper place.

"But our enquiries respecting the Religious persuasion to which Mr. Somerville belonged; having proved fruitless, we concluded to avoid everything that could give uneasiness to any American creed.

"The respected Remains, which Charles Barnet had from Auxerre, deposited in my house, was from there accompanied by the Consul, Mr. Barnet, and by Mr. Hawley of New York, by the Mayor of this Commune, several invited neighbors, a mourning concourse of people, and both of us, to a grave next to that where lies my Son's daughter.

"Although, uncertain as we were of his Religious persuasion, we made it a point of delicacy towards his family not to wish entering a Roman Catholic Church; we thought there was in one case an act of propriety, and no impropriety in every other case, to accept the offer of the Minister of the parish, to meet us on the ground and say those prayers to which no Protestant can have an objection.

"We are taking measures to become by an exchange, sole owners of the whole spot; thereby annexing it to the farm; when a grave, a plain monument, and an inscription will consecrate our affection and gratitude.

"And now, my dear Sir, it remains for me to apologize for those details, which, painful as they are, it has appeared necessary to lay before you and other members of the family. Should anything have been wanting unintentionally, in our performance with the advice of the American public officers here, what we have thought most consonant to your lamented Brother's and your own views; at least there has been no deficiency in our feelings; and in our eagerness on the deplorable occasion to do for the best.

"Be pleased to accept the affection, condolences, and high regard of two sympathizing friends, my Son and myself, to whom my whole family beg to be joined.

"Lafayette"

Another letter, written about a year after the preceeding, is as follows:

My Dear Sir:

"Your affectionate answer has afforded me a deep, though melancholy gratification.

"I shall ever lament the loss of your excellent Brother.

"Ever shall I remember with gratitude the wish he had expressed to connect his last Mansion with the Habitation of La Grange, and the assent you have been please to give to our arrangements.

"In consequence of an exchange made with the inhabitants of the Commune, under the sanction of the local and superior authorities, the Burying ground has become our family property, and a part of the estate; so that nothing can hereafter trouble us in the possession and management of it.

"That matter, I beg, you will kindly leave to us, and have the Honor to enclose a copy of the inscription in both languages.

"I beg, my Dear Sir, you will accept the best wishes and grateful regard of your sincere friend,

"Lafayette"

The inscription is:

William Clarke Somerville

"Citoyen des Etats Unis de l'Amerique du Nord Etat de Maryland, Representant du Gouvernement de son pays, pour une mission diplomatique, il mournt a Auxerre 5 Janvier, 1826.

"Citizen of the United States of North America, State of Maryland, while on a diplomatic mission from the Government of his Country, he departed this life at Auxerre, on the 5th of January, 1826.

"Il avait exprime le desir
d'etre inhume dans le lieu de
Sepulture des habitans de
La Grange."

"He had expressed a desire
to be interred in the burying
ground of the inhabitants of
La Grange.

"Ce voeu fut accompli avec
Reconnaissance le 19 Janvier,
1826, par son ami Le General
Lafayette."

"That kind wish has been grate-
fully fulfilled on the 19th of
January, by his friend, General
Lafayette."

In 1828, "Stratford Hall" was sold back to the Lee Family. In a letter from Henry Lee's nephew, L.T. O'Brien, to a member of the Tiernan family he wrote, "among the portraits and paintings I recall from Stratford Hall were one of George Washington by Gilbert Stuart, one of Payton Randolph, President of the first Continental Congress, and one of Lafayette—these three I bought. The one of Washington I sold for $200.00 to John B. Morris Sr. more than forty years ago, Randolph's was lost and Layafette I gave to my namesake, Brien Berry of San Francisco.

There were also portraits of Jane Shore, Nell Gwynn, and a woman in a nun's dress. These being acquired along with a quantity of silver from Light Horse Harry Lee when William Somerville purchased "Stratford Hall" in 1818."

With the death of William Somerville the succession of the American Somervells to the barony of Cambusnethan passed to John's brother James and his descendants, Susan Somervell's father, Thomas Truman Somervell being next in line.

James had married Susannah Dare probably of the same family as Virginia Dare, the first born baby of the Jamestown colony.

James, the second, lived at Stoakley, still standing on Hunting Creek on the east side of the Patuxent. The 1783 rent rolls show his brother John Somerville owned part of this tract. James prospered and letters show he made trips to Scotland as agent for the family fortunes.

His son James, the third, moved across the Patuxent where he owned a large plantation three miles north of Aquasco. He married Ann Magruder Truman, from a neighboring plantation. Ann's great-grandfather was Henry Truman, one of the four Truman brothers who were given large land grants in Southern Maryland in the 1660's. Henry was the only one to produce male descendants and it is said all bearing the name of Truman today are descended from Henry. A Calvert County history book says President Harry S. Truman is descended from this family.

During the Revolution, James, the third, lost an arm at Camden, South Carolina. He was a charter member of the Society of the Cincinnati. Cincinnatus was the Roman general who put down the sword for the plow. This organization was formed by veterans of the Revolution for the purpose of helping each other and those who had been wiped out by the war, and this is how Cincinnati, Ohio, was born. The organization continues today in Washington, D.C., with members consisting of descendents of oldest sons.

James' son and father of Susan Somervell, Thomas Truman Somervell, built the beautiful house "Greenwood" on his father's plantation. It was five stories high and honeycombed in the basement with rooms for house slaves. Here Susan Somervell was raised in high style on part of her grandfather's plantation with fourteen brothers and sisters. Years later a Weems cousin, after visiting her parents wrote "they had a large number of children and *all of them are independent*!" At the death of William Somervell the American succession to the Cambusnethan barony went to Thomas Truman Somervell, Susan Somervell's father.

It was from this plantation that Susan Somervell, her parents, and her grandparents attended "St. Paul's" church two miles up the road.

JOHN HANSON
The First President of the United States

The month following the Battle of Yorktown when we had at last won our independence, the Continental Congress met. Drawing up a constitution, the Articles of Confederation, John Hanson was named "The First President of the United States in Congress Assembled." George Washington wrote him to congratulate him on his appointment to "the highest office in the land," and it is probable that George Washington had a hand in his selection for a member of the Hanson family was the executor of George Washington's will. Although John Hanson was only President for one year he gave us our Judicial system, our Cabinet, our Postal System, and Thanksgiving Day. There were eight presidents before a new Constitution was drawn and George Washington became the first president to be elected by the people.

Portrait by Charles Wilson Peale, courtesy of the National Park Service

CHAPTER III   OF THE REVOLUTION AND A NEW COUNTRY

James, the third, who lost an arm during the Revolution at the Battle of Camden, South Carolina, fought with the famous Sixth Maryland Regiment which had a distinguished record in the South. It was surprising to find that three-fourths of the Revolution was fought in North and South Carolina.

In 1774 Maryland had already severed relations with England and the Proprietary Governor, Robert Eden, returned to England. So much did he love Maryland that after the Revolution he returned to live and is buried in the church yard of St. Anne's in the center of Annapolis.

In the late 1760's many prominent Southern Maryland families moved to Frederick, Maryland, among them John Hanson, to become the first President of the United States.

Many Marylanders are firm in their conviction that John Hanson was the First President of the United States, for one month after the Battle of Yorktown when we had at last achieved our independence, the Continental Congress met and drew up a Constitution, the Articles of Confederation, and named John Hanson, "The First President of the United States in Congress Assembled." Although he was only President for one year he had a rather remarkable record, for he gave us our Judicial System, our Cabinet, our Postal System and Thanksgiving Day. George Washington himself wrote and congratulated him on his "appointment to the highest office in the Land." There were eight presidents before a new constitution was drawn and George Washington became the first president to be elected by the people.

Thomas Johnson, who was to become the first Governor of Maryland, and Francis Scott Key's grandfather, also went to Frederick. Many were lawyers and there were probably two reasons for this settling. George Washington and his brother Lawrence had been given a large land grant in Ohio sometime before the Revolution and Frederick was a frontier town. It was also used as a route to Philadelphia. Iron foundries were now manufacturing much needed metal and a not too successful glass-making company was in operation. In any case, there is evidence that the practice of law here was most lucrative. But a most curious bit of history was to occur a hundred years later because of Frederick's ties to Southern Maryland.

It was during this period that the Stone family gave three great brothers to Maryland and American History. Perhaps the most famous of these was Thomas Stone, a signer of the Declaration of Independence from Maryland. (His wife was the sister of Dr. Gustavus Brown.) The rift with the "Mother Country" greatly saddened him and the affection for England must have remained with him until his death six years after the Revolution, for shortly before his death when he had fallen ill, he had on the advice to take a trip by Dr. Craik and Dr. Brown, chosen to visit England and as he waited for his ship at Alexandria, Virginia, he died. His home, Habre d'Aventure, an architectural gem near Port Tobacco, has recently been purchased by the U.S. Congress.

His brother John Hoskins Stone, fought as a Colonel in the Battles of Long Island, White Plains, Princeton and finally was so severely wounded at Germantown he was forced to resign. He was elected Governor of Maryland in 1794 and on appeal from George Washington gave financial aid for the building of government buildings in Washington.

The third brother, Michael Jenifer Stone, the father of Dr. Stone, was elected to the United States Congress in 1789 the same year Washington was elected President. While in Congress he voted for locating the

"MULBERRY GROVE"
Port Tobacco, Maryland

Birthplace of John Hanson, First President of the United States, it was named as a plantation designed to grow silk worms, but the project failed. During the Civil War it was headquarters for Union troops. The owners hid their chickens and animals deep in the woods during the occupation. The original house was destroyed by fire in the late 1920's but was faithfully reconstructed by Mrs. Richard Edelen and her many children who built the present house with their own hands.

B. Taussig '8?

seat of the government at Washington, D.C. Later he became a Judge of the Circuit Court of Charles County. Here he built "Equality" near LaPlata shortly after the Battle of Yorktown when everyone went around saying "At last we have equality."

Our family has a letter to Judge Stone from George Washington. Between 1783 and 1789 after George Washington had resigned his commission and before he had become President of the United States he had in his retirement become president of the building of the C&O Canal, then called the Potomac Company. Apparently Judge Stone had written to General Washington telling him of rumors that the enterprise was having financial difficulties and asking him for the status of the stock he had invested in the company. George Washington's reply was to the affect that there were financial problems and what he might expect as a return of some of his money.

Daniel of St. Thomas Jenifer, nephew of John Hanson, and uncle of the three Stone brothers, found himself in a dilemma. For years he had been in the service of the Lord Proprietor, as a member of the Provincial Court, and the commission to settle boundary disputes with Pennsylvania and Delaware. Under the last two proprietors he had held office as the Proprietor's Agent and Receiver General in charge of Proprietary Revenues. When he sided with the Revolutionists, almost all of them had been former political enemies in quarrels with the Proprietor. He was made President of the State Senate in 1777 and the following year he was elected to the Continental Congress where he took a stand against issuing paper money. In 1782 he was Intendant of Maryland Revenues and Financial Agent of the State. In 1787 he went to the Constitutional Convention and signed the Constitution of the United States for Maryland. My grandson and I, on a trip to the Hall of Records in Annapolis, were startled to find in the corner of the entrance hall an exhibit of Kunta Kinte of "Roots." A copy of the Maryland Gazette showed Daniel of St. Thomas Jenifer as the agent for the cargo of slaves of which Kunta Kinte was one. Daniel's sister, Elizabeth, was Dr. Stone's grandmother.

One of the least known but one of the greatest patriots of the Revolution whose life in America began in Maryland was Robert Morris. He had come at the age of fourteen to join his father at Oxford, Maryland, on the Eastern Shore. His father was a shipping agent who a year after his son's arrival was killed in an unfortunate accident while firing a gun to celebrate the arrival of a ship from England. The gun misfired.

Young Robert Morris went to Philadelphia as an apprentice to a banker. By the time he was twenty-one his financial genius had won him a partnership in the bank and he was soon to become one of the richest men in the colonies.

Robert Morris financed much of the Revolution including the "Crossing of the Delaware" and the "Battle of Yorktown" but Congress never paid him the million dollars it owed him and he was thrown into debtor's prison. George Washington, in Philadelphia to receive a citation from the Congress, turned down a banquet in his honor to dine with his close friend in jail.

The Robert Morris Inn where the great patriot lived in Oxford is all that Marylanders have as a monument to this remarkable man.

Here boaters congregate in this charming town in the summer months unmindful of what we owe to his memory. Who knows for whom the Morris chair was named?

Margaret Stone of Habre de Venture gave all of Thomas Stone's letters and papers to Dr. Stone's son, Tom. Among them were four letters from Robert Morris.

When Habre de Venture was first sold out of the family and restored, the new owner found brown paper stuffed in a broken window pane in the attic. This turned out to be a rough draft of the Constitution of Maryland.

At the end of the 18th Century after the Revolution, for a decade Catholics in Maryland were severely persecuted again. The Catholic Bishop John Carroll, who was the first consecrated Catholic Bishop in the United States, was forced to hold secret masses in the attic of his home in Annapolis.

At this time, a large number of Catholics left Maryland for Kentucky with the purpose of setting up a new country with a king under the auspices of France, since this was before the Louisiana Purchase. The plan fell through, but this is how Louisville, Kentucky was born, and why, because of the War of 1812 and this emigration, Kentucky has so many family ties to Maryland.

"ST. PAUL'S"—1733
Baden, Maryland

This was the parish of Thomas John Claggett after his consecration in New York as the first Episcopal bishop consecrated in the United States. It is unique in that it is the only church known to have a sundial embedded in a church wall. This one is over the front entrance. Built in 1733, it still has the communion silver service given by Queen Anne.

The British rode their horses into this church the summer of 1814 on their return from Washington and smashed the baptismal font. It was sent to England for repairs and the metal ring holding it together may still be seen today.

Susan Somervell, her parents, and her grandparents all attended this church.

B. Taussig '82

ST. Paul's 1733
Baden, Md.

BRITISH MARCH TO BURN WASHINGTON 1814

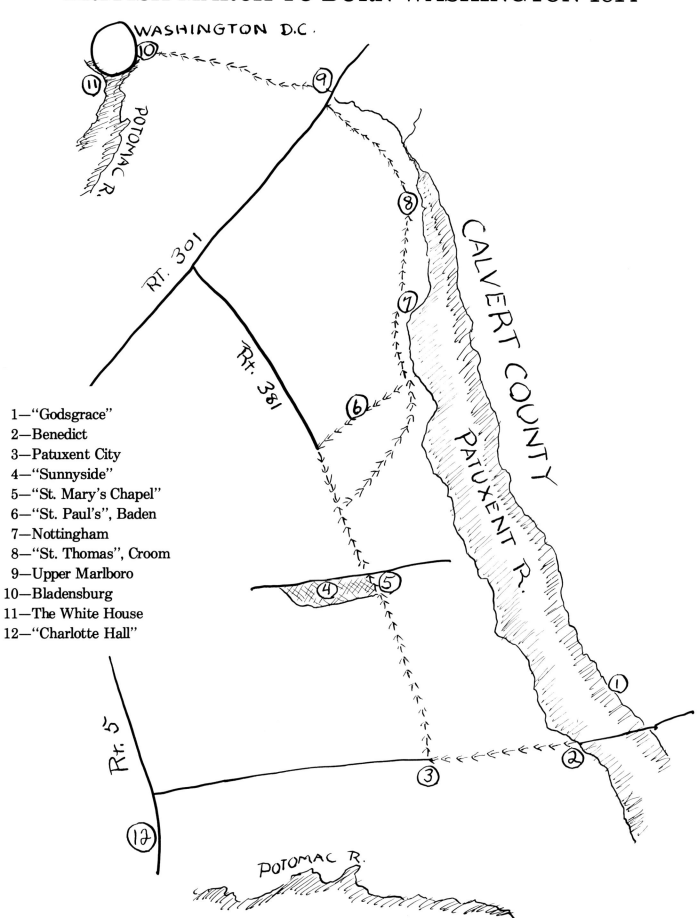

1—"Godsgrace"
2—Benedict
3—Patuxent City
4—"Sunnyside"
5—"St. Mary's Chapel"
6—"St. Paul's", Baden
7—Nottingham
8—"St. Thomas", Croom
9—Upper Marlboro
10—Bladensburg
11—The White House
12—"Charlotte Hall"

CHAPTER V   THE WAR OF 1812—HURRAY FOR BALTIMORE

Following the Revolution the British attempted to maintain control of the seas. Then, as it is today, it was imperative to keep the sea lanes open for import and export. Periodic raids by the British on the coast and engagements at sea continued until 1812 when the United States Congress voted for war. The British gathered a large force and in 1813 entered the Chesapeake Bay for revenge and the ultimate purpose of destroying the shipbuilding, particularly at Baltimore. The Baltimore clippers, rigged fore and aft, could outrace and outmaneuver the square-rigged ships of the British and by 1812 the Baltimore clippers had accounted for 556 British vessels, one-third of all the British ships sunk. The London newspapers stormed, "the inhabitants of Baltimore must be punished with the weapons that shook the turrets of Copenhagen!"

The British harassed the Eastern Shore with raids on plantations and towns. The town of St. Michaels is proud of its citizens' plan to thwart an attack when its inhabitants, while underfire, turned out all the town lights and hung lanterns in the tree tops causing the British to overshoot the village.

As winter approached, the British made their headquarters on little Tangier Island. This may have caused the ultimate defeat of the British for being barely above sea level the drinking water was contaminated, the loss of life was high, and the survivors were seriously weakened by dysentery.

Our country was sadly lacking in either an adequate army or combatant ships in the face of the largest force to ever attack the United States. Commodore Joshua Barney had 13 shallow draft barges built in Baltimore to be rowed by 20 men with 24 pound guns mounted on the bow. By June of 1814 the barges were in fierce combat with the British. No match for the enemy fleet they nevertheless accounted for much damage and were able to keep them at bay until Admiral Cockburn arrived. Then sailing up the Patuxent savage raids began on the towns and plantations. Setting fire to warehouses at Huntingtown, in Calvert County, soon the whole town was in flames. Gone rapidly were the old County Seat of Calvert County, part of old Prince Frederick, and many beautiful plantation homes were destroyed including "Godsgrace," home of the grandparents of President Zachery Taylor's wife, whose daughter was to become the first wife of Jefferson Davis. The raids and the plundering went on in the lower part of the Potomac as well until over 300 plantation owners from Southern Maryland, their homes gone, their crops burned, and stripped of their livestock, picked up lock, stock and barrel and left for a little town called Bardstown, Kentucky, where many ancient Maryland names are still to be found.

In August of 1814, British reinforcements arrived from Bermuda bringing 7,000 more veteran soldiers and marines and more armed warships making the total of enemy troops more than 20,000 men. They congregated at Benedict, seven miles from Aquasco, and began the march to Washington. Marching up what is now Route 381 they passed "Sunnyside" and went on to Upper Marlboro where they used the home of Dr. Beanes as headquarters, and then on to Bladensburg.

At the White House, Dolly Madison found herself alone with only a servant, the President having gone to Bladensburg to be with the troops. Carefully removing the portrait of George Washington by Gilbert Stuart from its frame, she rolled it up and disguising herself in old clothes fled in a wagon with the cherished possession across the Potomac and into Virginia.

Undaunted at Bladensburg the British marched to the White House setting it afire. Fortunately a violent storm came up soon thereafter, the deluge extinguishing the fire before the White House was totally destroyed.

On the way back to Benedict the British again used Dr. Beanes' house as headquarters. In a bookcase at "Sunnyside" I found an extraordinary book of "Heretofore Unpublished Poems" by Francis Scott Key, published in 1857 by friends and relatives. What was so remarkable was the introduction by Roger Brooke Taney, his brother-in-law, who was to become famous for an opinion upholding a slave holders' rights in the Dred Scott case as Chief Justice of the Supreme Court during the Civil War.

In his introduction he relates the step by step account of Francis Scott Key's role in the attack on Baltimore and the subsequent writing of the "Star Spangled Banner."

When the British left Upper Marlboro and their headquarters at Dr. Beanes, Dr. Beanes, who was Francis Scott Key's cousin, joined a posse and rounded up British stragglers, throwing them in jail. The British, considering Dr. Beanes had broken parole, returned and took him prisoner. Francis Scott Key went to Washington and secured a request for his release from President Madison and on joining the British fleet on the lower Potomac received an agreement to his release. However, to insure that plans to attack Baltimore would remain secret both he and Dr. Beanes would be held until after the attack.

When the British fleet arrived at Baltimore, Baltimore was ready and as the British general (the same General Ross who had led the attack on Washington) stepped ashore he was shot and killed and the plan of attack fell through. The enemy then turned their guns on Fort McHenry. As Francis Scott Key watched through a porthole through the night he knew that as long as those guns were firing from Fort McHenry we had not lost. At dawn the British straggled back to the ship with the news of defeat. Francis Scott Key took out an envelope and wrote the glorious "Star Spangled Banner" on the back and on the following day after his release he took it to a friend in Baltimore who was so enthralled he made over a thousand copies.

What was so delightful about the introduction was the end where Chief Justice Taney wrote "It may not always be our National Song but it will always be the Song of Maryland." And he was wrong on both counts!

As the British returned to their ships from Upper Marlboro they came back on the Croom Road, cutting across to Baden where they entered the lovely old church of "St. Paul's" and smashed the baptismal font. Later it was sent back to England for repair and the metal ring around the top may still be seen today.

There is no doubt the British burned other homes and plantations on their way back to Benedict. I think it is possible that they burned a house standing where "Sunnyside" is today and Dr. Stone attached his house to the remaining outside kitchen. An 1826 deed mentions only out-buildings but no house.

In British accounts they contemptuously write of empty homes on their march and accuse the men of Southern Maryland of being cowards, but records show that every able-bodied man from the Aquasco area had already left to defend Washington, Susan Somervell's father among them.

"OLD WHITE HOUSE"—1803
Charlotte Hall, Maryland

This is the only old building left standing of Charlotte Hall, a once handsome institution. Commissioned to be built in 1774 as the first military preparatory school in the United States it continued until 1976. In the early days it was well attended by young men from the Northern Neck of Virginia as well as Southern Maryland.

A company of students tried to engage the British on their march in 1814 but were no match for the seasoned soldiers who had just defeated Napoleon's troops.

Among its famous students were Admiral Raphael Semmes, Chief Justice Roger Brooke Taney, George Waterson, the first Librarian of Congress, Edward Bates, attorney to President Lincoln, called by Horace Greely the most brilliant orator of his day, and J.M.S. Causin, who John Quincy Adams called the most talented man in the U.S. Congress.

At the 1890 Reunion over 40 of the alumni present had served in the U.S. Congress.

Both of Dr. Stone's sons went there, and Dr. Stone's grandfather was a founder.

B. Taussig '83

CHAPTER V   A LOST RELATIVE AND TEXAS

Anna Lee had often passed family lore and history along to me. Once she said we had an Alexander Somervell in the family she could not account for. One day in the attic I found an interesting box of correspondence.

In 1935 a Mr. Kemp, writing a history of Texas, had written to the Postmaster of Aquasco to ask if anyone in the village knew of the family background of an Alexander Somervell, his will having been probated in Texas in 1850 in which he named Aquasco as his birthplace, his father as James Somervell, and Elizabeth MacGruder as his mother. Alexander Somervell, Mr. Kemp wrote, had fought in the battle of San Jacinto eventually becoming a general in the Texas Army and subsequently becoming Secretary of War under President Burnet when Texas was an independent country. He founded a town, Saluria, in Texas but died in a strange way. Carrying a large sum of money in a boat to Saluria, the boat was found overturned, he was lashed to the mast, and the money was gone. Other correspondence showed he was Susan Somervell's uncle, or the younger half-brother of her father, who because of the English custom of inheritance to the oldest son had gone to seek his own fortune, thus disappearing from the lives of his Southern Maryland relatives.

Walter Colton, the Chaplain, ran California during the three years of battle with the Mexicans until the final acquisition by the United States. The portrait of him in Colton Hall, Monterey, California was painted from this miniature found in Dr. Stone's attic.

CHAPTER VI   WALTER COLTON, THE NAVY AND CALIFORNIA

In 1825, another great-great grandfather, William Colton, came to King George in the Northern Neck of Virginia marrying Anna Saunders, a first cousin of James Madison, probably coming in some capacity with the administration of John Quincy Adams. He and his brother, Walter, were from Georgia, Vermont not far from the Canadian border on Lake Champlain.

In another box in the attic I found a box of old photographs, a beautiful miniature of a young man perhaps made in the 1820's and a book published in 1850 by Walter Colton titled "Three Years in California."

Walter Colton was the uncle of my great-grandfather, Walter Colton. I sat down in the attic and began to read one of the most enchanting tales I have ever read by a great master of prose.

In 1846 the Californios had convened and had decided that they would like to become a part of the United States. They comprised many nationalities: English, Russian, Scottish and American in addition to Spanish. Although I was raised in the Navy I never knew before this moment that California was a Navy acquisition. Commodore Sloat, having been given a go ahead by the American Government, had put up an American flag at San Francisco and another at Monterey. At this time Commodore Stockton called in Walter Colton, a Navy chaplain, and told him that he was to be the appointed Alcalde (Mayor) of Monterey, the headquarters of the operation. This would make him the highest judicial authority, the senior administrator, and the senior Alcalde of all Alcaldes.

Walter Colton was less than enthusiastic and suggested that the ship's doctor or the purser might be better qualified, but the Commodore said they were needed aboard ship.

Walter Colton packed his little suitcase and went to the home of Mr. Larkin, the American Consul, where he had a room. He became a great admirer of Mr. Larkin and at a later date would have wished him to accept a role in government when California became a state.

A man with a marvelous sense of humor and a lyrical gift with words, Walter then began his journal. On uneventful official days, which were not many, he recounts trivial local incidents that give color to the people and illuminate those three years.

Then the battles with the Mexicans began, mostly around Los Angeles and San Diego. Descriptions of sailors who had never ridden a horse, being mounted and doing battle with swords against the Mexicans, who had ridden before they walked and carried lances, would have been funny if it had not been a temporary setback. Prize ships were brought into Monterey from Mazatlan.

The people of Monterey opened their homes and their hearts to the American Chaplain and, two months after his arrival, elected him their own Alcalde before the completion of the acquisition.

At the end of May 1848 he wrote, "Our town was startled out of its dreams today by the announcement that gold had been discovered on American Fork." In June 1848 he wrote, "Another report reached us this morning from American Fork. The rumor ran that several workmen . . . had thrown up shining scales of yellow ore, that proved to be gold."

By mid-July the servants had joined the gold rush and the Chaplain was cooking his own breakfast. In

September the Chaplain went to American Fork (next to Sutter's Creek) to see and report for himself. He described 50,000 people milling around with picks and finding gold everywhere.

The price of flour rose to $400 a barrel and, hold onto your hat, interest rates soared to an incredible 26%. Monterey became a town of gambling and prostitution overnight. Being the only Protestant clergyman in California, Walter Colton took a puritan view of these activities.

Early in his administration he had started the first newspaper in California. Finding an old printing press from a decaying mission he repaired it and, having no paper, he used cigar paper with which Californios wrapped their cigars. This first newspaper was an overnight success with a weekly circulation of 2,800.

He had immediately instituted a very successful prison reform, where prisoners were used as a work force but were paid for their work. In 1848 the Chaplain started a town hall with the lower apartments to be used for the first school house in California. Built by the labor of paid prisoners and mostly paid for by fines from his gambling friends it was called "the finest building in the West."

In recent years much attention has been given to the plate theory of the crust of the earth. Only a few years ago, a young woman archeologist found an ancient whale skeleton near the top of the Sierras, the plate theory making its location reasonable, but Walter Colton wrote, "let him (the geologist) turn inland and he will find on the mountains, two hundred miles from the sea and on elevations of a thousand feet the same marine products; and not only these, but the skeleton of a whale almost entire. How came that monster up there, high and dry, glimmering like the pale skeleton of a huge cloud between us and the moon?"

At the end of his book, he lists prominent citizens and their contributions. His book is dedicated to Gen. Mariano Guadalupe Vallejo. He says of him, "His father had held a military command under the crown of Spain but in his discontent with Mexican rule he not only assisted in the acquisition by the United States but, as a very rich man, gave to the United States some 14 different parcels of land for government buildings including hospitals, schools, and orphanages." He also gave nearly half a million dollars (a sizeable amount in those days) in some 22 different amounts for the building of public buildings.

At the end of the book Colton lists towns with descriptions and predictions for the future. Of San Francisco he said, "Three years ago only a dozen shanties sprinkled its hills . . . now it looks like the skeleton of a huge city."

He had a great love for the California missions. He wrote, "In 1833 the supreme government of Mexico issued a decree which converted them into civil institutions subject to the control of the state . . . the civil administrators plundered them." Taking each mission, he gives a list of inventory prior to 1833 and compares it to what existed 16 years later when he wrote his book. Of the Mission of Dolores at San Francisco he wrote, "Its stock in 1825 consisted of 76,000 head of cattle, 950 tame horses, 2000 breeding mares, 84 stud of choice breed, 820 mules, 79,000 sheep, 2000 hogs, 450 yoke of working oxen, 18,000 bushels of wheat, $35,000 in merchandize, and $25,000 in specie. It was secularized in 1834 by order of Gen. Figueroa and soon became a wreck." Contrary to common belief, the Indians loved the beauty and prosperity of the missions. In only one case was a padre cruel, and he was recalled to Spain. Each mission had a similar accounting to that of Dolores.

When the town hall-school house was completed, it was used for the Constitutional Convention to make California a state in 1849. Named Colton Hall, it is now the Historical Center for California and the City Hall of Monterey.

Last Christmas my husband and I went to California. On a special side trip to Monterey we visited Colton Hall. At the end of the great hall was a beautiful portrait of Walter Colton—and there to my unbelieving eyes was the one and the same as my beautiful miniature from the attic whose identity I had not known until that moment. In piecing it together my great-grandfather Colton had had two portraits commissioned by a New York painter in 1911, one of his uncle from the miniature, and one of himself. The one of my great-grandfather hangs in the dining room of my farm house but the miniature I have given to the museum at Colton Hall.

"COLTON HALL"—1849

Monterey, California

Built in 1849 with prison labor and paid for with fines from the gamblers of the gold rush, it was known at that time as "the finest building in the West." Finished in time to hold the convention to make California a state, it is now the City Hall of Monterey and the Historical Center for California.

The upper floor was built as a large meeting hall, while the rooms on the first floor were built for a school house—the first in California.

CHAPTER VII   THE CIVIL WAR AND A FAMILY UP TO ITS NECK IN CONFEDERATE INTRIGUE

At about the same time Alexander Somervell was helping to make history in Texas, Dr. Stone married Susan Somervell in 1844 whom he had met in the garden of his relatives at "Sotterly," which was at that time a girl's school for friends and relatives of the Briscoe family.

He built "Sunnyside" for his bride adding it on to an 18th Century outdoor kitchen with a hyphen between the two buildings to be used as his office. The out buildings included an ice house twenty feet deep, filled in January from the creek below, a summer kitchen, slave quarters with a schoolroom above, a meat or a smoke house, a corn crib, a stable, and a barn.

The house itself had a center hall, a large dining room, living room, and upstairs, two large bedrooms, all with fireplaces. Later the roof was raised to add two small bedrooms in the attic as the family grew.

"Sunnyside" is called an historic house by Prince George's County "for the family that lived there and as an excellent example of mid-19th century architecture." A delight to carpenters, the square nails and strong construction can keep one exploring for hours.

The 18th Century outdoor kitchen was used as a winter kitchen by the family. This small building included a pantry and a root cellar. An attic above has windows suggesting a house slave slept there. The ceiling is so constructed with beams and boards that the trap door is undetectable. It is here that Anna Lee said the family silver was hidden during the Civil War. Recently the large fireplace was unbricked to reveal two iron arms on which pots were hanged and a huge iron square weighing perhaps three hundred pounds which had been used at the back of the fireplace to store heat. This dates the kitchen to 1740 or before.

Conveyances consisted of a buggy, a Danby (something like a surrey) and a wagon used among other things to bring supplies from the Baltimore boat at Truman's Point on the Patuxent once a month.

Meals were prompt and members of the family were groomed and dressed for breakfast at 8 o'clock. Each member had daily tasks for the maintenance of the household. The main meal was in the middle of the day, at which time it was not unusual to see at least six vegetables. My mother tells me that every family had the magic number of exactly six silver serving spoons. Ancient family recipes provided for delicious meals and until recent times the most treasured Christmas present was a country ham cured at "Sunnyside" by a two hundred year old family recipe.

Pork and fowl were the domestic staples and beef was only included in the diet when brought by visiting guests, for to kill cattle for a small family with no way to safely store it was not practical.

Visiting relatives was the main social event for the older family members. Arriving without notice, they frequently stayed for as long as a month. Several trundle beds I found attested to a gregarious people.

The young ladies gave parties in honor of visiting cousins or friends, but church was where the budding young people made the initial contact and great care was given by the young girls to be the prettiest, and slyly look to see who might notice them. In a diary, I was amused to read that one beau came only every New Year's Eve to court one of Dr. Stone's daughters.

During the spring and summer months the great social event for the young people was the tournament. The winner crowned the "Queen of Love and Beauty" and the participating "knights" chose their "princesses" for the court. All of this excitement was followed by a ball. This custom has been handed down from the Normans and jousting is still the official sport of Maryland.

Baltimore, though much further away than Washington, was considered to be more elegant and a city of high fashion. Gowns and hats were purchased here and to visit in this culturally glamorous town was cause for great excitement.

Certain customs have been carried from generation to generation—Christmas customs in particular. Although the Christmas tree is a mid-19th Century German addition to the holiday ceremony in Maryland, other unique customs such as shooting fireworks Christmas day date back to the 17th Century and continue today although the reason has long been forgotten. In the early days, plantation owners fired a cannon Christmas morning—their way of saying "Merry Christmas" to friends on neighboring plantations perhaps a mile away.

Early settlers burned a yule log Christmas Eve, partying as long as the log lasted. Slaves were given rum for their own party and they too partied for as long as the yule log lasted. Needless to say, the search for the biggest yule log was the name of the game.

In our family, plum pudding is traditional with the added ceremony of soft custard in cups without handles placed around the center of the table.

Teasing and secrets lead up to the great day with an almost unbearable tension. Festive decorating goes on everywhere and cooking and cooking and cooking until Christmas morning at dawn, members of the family try to be first to cry "Christmas Gift" which obligates a present to the crier.

Dr. Stone had seven children, six of whom lived to maturity. His oldest daughter, Mary, was the only one to marry, and at her death, her two small girls were raised at "Sunnyside."

The older son, Tom, ran "Sunnyside" farm and farmed "Habre de Venture" for his much older cousin Margaret. It was to him she gave all of Thomas Stone, the Signer's, letters and papers including four letters from Robert Morris—all of which were later sold to the Library of Congress.

The second daughter, known to all of us as "Auntie," was firey and fun-loving. She was to run the kitchen and the household. It was she who taught me as a little girl to curl my hair glamorously with rags and in my teens would call to ask about all of my beaux, for, as she put it, "all of mine are dead." Occasionally, she was a mild source of embarrassment such as the time she left an empty bottle at a private girls' school for me to take home to be filled by my father with her medicinal whiskey. I remember her at ninety being ever so careful not to wear a dress that was too "old" for her.

Every night in the privacy of her room she would "crimp" her hair. This consisted of weaving the hair back and forth on huge hairpins. I only saw this once for to appear before anyone with "crimped" hair would have been comparable today with "streaking."

"Auntie" and two other village spinsters embroidered the beautiful altar cloth at St. Mary's Chapel, for fine needlework was part of every young lady's training. Recently, the altar cloth was repaired at the Washington Cathedral, one of the few places where the art remains. "Auntie" was to raise her sister Mary's two daughters and her two granddaughters, Anna Lee and my mother.

The third daughter, "Terrie," taught school at the village. A letter from a friend to her mother says, "I had tea with Terrie yesterday. I do not know how she does all she does and entertains as much as she does. The Stones are always entertaining and the house is always full of company."

The youngest daughter, "Nell," went to Washington to work for the government. This was something of an embarrassment to the family for only a few occupations were acceptable for ladies. (Work in a bank or a library, or running a boarding house would have been considered suitable for a gentlewoman.) Nevertheless it was "Nell" to whom the motherless Anna Lee was the closest.

Manumission papers show that Dr. Stone had 10 slaves, 7 of whom were Lucy Glascoe and her six adult children. Family letters refer to another slave as the beloved "Mom" Beck as nurse and "mother" to the children. The only apparent difference that freedom made to slaves in this household was that a former slave from across the road, known as "Uncle Watt," came to Dr. Stone and asked if it were true that he was free and when Dr. Stone replied that he was, "Uncle Watt" then asked if he could work for Dr. Stone. He was taken in with wages of $5 a month. Since Dr. Stone's farm was small and only for family maintenance, his slaves were part of the family. They simply remained after the Civil War and Becky's granddaughter, "Katie," was, in Anna Lee's own words, "the only real mother I ever knew," Anna Lee's own mother having died at her birth.

But up the road at "Greenwood," where Susan Somervell was born and raised in style with fourteen brothers and sisters, it was a different story. For theirs was a large plantation sweeping to the Patuxent River, dependent on wide scale planting and the export of tobacco to England for prosperity and the more than one hundred slaves it took to maintain such a plantation were no longer productive. Humanity required that they be allowed to live on the land but with no jobs and nowhere to go, they simply remained. Five years after the Civil War, "Greenwood" was sold. An older villager says that she remembers the coachman from "Greenwood" who came to work for her family. Two coach lamps from "Greenwood" adorn either side of the door at "Sunnyside."

Life for seventeen years continued happily and prosperously until the Civil War.

Two years after Dr. Stone built "Sunnyside," Walter Colton, the Chaplain, was to arrive at Monterey, California, on the U.S. Congress.

Dr. Stone practiced medicine, but he was also an Examiner of Schools for Prince George's County. Shortly before the Civil War, he had hired a teacher for his children, Emily Colton. "Aunt Nina" Colton, as she was called, was a niece of Walter Colton, the Chaplain, and was to be, I am sure, a pivotal point for a family role in an extraordinary Civil War story.

My mother had been raised at "Sunnyside" by her grandmother's sister, "Auntie," who was 8 years old when the Civil War broke out. Perhaps no part of the South had taken such a beating as Southern Maryland and the Northern Neck of Virginia, and my mother had had a first hand account of the horrors experienced by every Southern Maryland family.

My father's grandfather, on the other hand, had fought for the Union. My father was a sea-going warrior and there was no doubt who ruled our family, but when the Civil War was mentioned my mother would draw herself up, defend Mrs. Surratt staunchly, curl her lip at the mention of Lincoln, and bears a life-time shame for having been born in New York where her father just happened to be in business. It was the only battle I ever knew my father not to fight.

My father's grandfather had been on the "Kearsarge" that had sunk the famous "Alabama" off Cherbourg, France. The "Alabama" under the command of the famous Confederate Admiral Raphael Semmes, had accounted for 58 Union ships before she had met her demise.

In the early 1950's my father, as Chief of Naval Operations, was to give the commissioning address to a new "Alabama" at Norfolk, Virginia. Valuing his life, he was very careful not to mention his grandfather's role in the end of that first great "Alabama."

Franklin Buchanan, another great Scot from Baltimore, devised the plan for the United States Naval Academy. So beautifully planned that his principles are still applied today at that fine institution, he was to become its first superintendent. At the outbreak of the Civil War he resigned his Commission and became the senior naval officer in the Confederate Navy. At Hampton Roads, Virginia, when the Monitor met the Merrimac (renamed the "Virginia"), Admiral Buchanan was wounded and was not active in the engagement the following day when the "Virginia" sank the U.S. Congress, that very ship that had taken Walter Colton, the Chaplain, to Monterey 16 years before. The "Virginia" sank two other ships in this engagement.

The North was primarily industrial, while the South was agricultural, marketing their cotton and tobacco crops abroad in exchange for foreign goods. In addition, when the South began to build their own cotton mills using slave labor it put an economic squeeze on the North and there was pressure on the government to put high tarriffs on imported goods to increase trade with the North. John Quincy Adams for some thirty-five years had been vociferous on the subject of abolition, for the North was suffering economically by the self-contained prosperity of the South. By 1857 the North was in a deep depression and northern industrialists were bearing down on slavery.

In any case, when national elections were held in 1860 Abraham Lincoln, who was basically a moderate on the question of slavery, had nevertheless run on a platform of high tariffs. But the real fear was the Republican party for no Southerner had ever voted for anyone other than a Democrat.

South Carolina kept its state legislature in session pending the outcome of the election and on December 20th 1860 seceded from the Union.

In Southern Maryland, Charles County had formed a committee to determine what to do about the one vote given to Lincoln. It was resolved the voter should be politely invited to leave the county and another committee of three was formed to make sure he went. Across the bay, Queen Anne County gave not one vote to Lincoln so great was the fear of the Republican party.

In January of 1861, 10,000 Union troops were marched into Charles County by President Buchanan who like Lincoln supported states rights to hold slaves but was determined at all costs to preserve the Union. By the time of Lincoln's Inauguration in March, seven states had already seceded from the Union.

That Lincoln was a moderate on slavery and in the beginning supported the states right to determine the slave issue is evident by the following portion of his Inaugural Address: "Apprehension seems to exist among the people of the southern states, that by the accession of a Republican administration, their property and their peace, and personal security are to be endangered . . . I have no purpose directly or indirectly to interfere with the institution of slavery in the states where it exists . . . we denounce the lawless invasion by armed force of the soil of any state or territory, no matter under what pretext, as among the gravest of crimes." This was on March 4, 1861, one month before the Confederacy fired on Fort Sumpter.

But Lincoln had inherited a problem that was well underway long before his presidency began.

Maryland, in the south where the land is flat, was agricultural with a plantation economy but north of Baltimore, where the land becomes hilly and even mountainous, the state becomes more industrial so Southern Maryland and the Eastern Shore were in sympathy with the Confederate cause and Northern Maryland sided with the Union.

As Maryland prepared to vote on secession with enough votes to secede Lincoln seized the legislature and prevented this, and every able-bodied Southern Maryland man or boy jumped across the Potomac to Virginia to join the Confederacy.

Already seven states had seceded and two months before Lincoln's Inauguration the preceeding administration had sent ten thousand troops into tiny little Charles County—Charles County, the county that gave us so many glorious men in the forming of our country during the Revolution and in the creation of the United States, and now was to become a stage for one of the greatest tragedies of our history.

Many Southerners themselves deplored slavery. General Robert E. Lee himself wrote his wife in 1857, "In this enlightened age, there are few, I believe, but will acknowledge that slavery as an institution is a moral and a political evil in any country . . . I think however it a greater evil to the white than to the black race . . . the blacks are better off here than in Africa, morally, socially, and physically . . . their emancipation will sooner result from the mild and melting influence of Christianity than the storms and tempest of firey controversy." Of the Abolitionists he further worte, "Is it not strange that the descendants of those Pilgrim fathers who crossed the Atlantic to preserve their own freedom of opinion have always proved themselves intolerant of the spiritual liberty of others?" And so it was that a President who approved states rights to hold slaves and a great general who deplored slavery were to go to war flying banners of causes in opposition to their beliefs.

Maryland itself had outlawed the importation of slaves nearly one hundred years before the Civil War.

I think it is fair to say that most slaves were well-treated. I even read that in the 18th Century a law was passed to prohibit slave owners from forcing slaves to eat terrapin or wild duck more than once a week! But certainly there were cruel slave owners. Such an owner was one who owned Josiah Henson of Charles County. He escaped to Canada and became a Methodist minister in 1830, and it was he who Harriet Beecher Stowe used as a model for Uncle Tom in her book, "Uncle Tom's Cabin."

But there is much evidence that, for the most part, slaves were well-treated.

In Walter Colton's treasure box was a charming small book by a former slave, Joseph Walker from Spotsylvania, Virginia. The book had been dictated to the minister of St. George's Church at Fredericksburg, Virginia, where Joseph had become the beloved sexton during his latter days.

He starts his story at the house across from the Court House in Spotsylvania where his master gathers the family and the slaves together to tell them he is leaving to join the Confederacy. Shortly thereafter, fighting breaks out on the front lawn of the house and Joseph, then only eight years old, flees into the woods with the family, the master's baby in his arms. When the fighting subsides he and his mother help his mistress pack the family silver and she departs for the South with her family. Joseph and his mother went several miles away to a safer place for the duration of the war.

The tender loving relationship between these slaves and their owners is never more beautifully revealed then when, after the Civil War, Joseph, as a free man prospering with ten acres of land, makes a loan to his former master to help him back on his feet.

A full page article in the Fredericksburg newspaper during the 1920's honors Joseph Walker with his life story and achievements as a beloved and important part of the Fredericksburg scene.

On discovering a museum at Spotsylvania next to the Court House, I drove there to visit and to give it the little book, for I knew that that was where it belonged. It was here that I met the delightful Judge Francis Waller who owns and operates the museum. It was he who told me that it was his family, the Waller family, who had purchased Kunta Kinte of "Roots." The Waller family was closely enough related to Walter Colton's family for Walter's oldest sister to have been named Rosalie Waller.

In July of 1861 President Lincoln had removed the Maryland legislature to Frederick, where as the known secessation legislators arrived by train they were seized and thrown in jail—this less than four months after Lincoln's Inaugural Address in which he said, "we denounce the lawless invasion by armed force of the soil or territory no matter under what pretext, as among the gravest of crimes."

At the first roll call not one legislator appeared. Only legislators supporting the Union were permitted to participate and this was how Maryland became part of the Union. There are still those who would have liked to have had what they consider the honor of seceding.

That same July, Lincoln invaded Virginia. The ladies from Washington packed picnics and sat on the grassy knolls of nearby Virginia to watch the battle as if it were some form of entertainment but it wasn't long before they knew it was war and they fled to their carriages and back to Washington.

In Charles County, Southern Marylanders were particularly bitter for the 20,000 troops that were occupying this small county by December had created havoc and devastation. In December of 1861, the Port Tobacco Times reported "twenty thousand troops are stationed upon the soil of Charles County, we are told to protect us from the Rebels and yet we are exposed to more danger, to more losses and damage or at least as much as if these very Rebels were here. Our farms are deprived of their provender to such an extent that the cattle must die, our citizens are deprived of homes almost and fences farms and fields fall prey to the ruthless hands of those very friends who come here to protect us."

"Our negroes—ah, this is the point—our negroes, are taken from us time and again, with no remuneration and threats of violence if we seek to recover them."

At this point the Proclamation of Emancipation had not yet been given. Dr. Stone had 10 slaves and my mother says they hid in the woods when Union troops came for the men were seized and conscripted into the Union army, without free choice.

The English had freed their slaves in 1825 paying owners $400 per slave and creating a probationary period to make the transaction run smoothly. At one point President Lincoln had made such a proposal to Congress but Congress had turned it down.

In Maryland the balance of slaves was just about one half of the negro population, many Marylanders having already freed their slaves.

When the Proclamation finally came two years after the war had begun it freed only the slaves of the belligerent states but the four states that did not secede were not included. It was the hope that the Proclamation would encourage Confederate states to withdraw and join the Union in order to continue to hold slaves.

President Lincoln's firmness in his desire to preserve the Union was not enough to inspire the Union troops to combat. Flying the banner of the moral issue of slavery was a necessary crusade to rally a force that had 200,000 deserters, and so it was that a President that believed in the states rights to hold slaves found himself on the side of a fight to abolish slavery, while a great man and a great general who abhorred slavery found himself the leader in the fight to preserve slavery and an existing way of life.

And so poor Charles County from the beginning found herself victimized without having given cause.

On the Maryland side of the mouth of the Potomac is Point Lookout, a Union prison camp, that held 25,000 brutally treated prisoners.

Conditions were so grim at Point Lookout the last year of the war, that General Lee finally decided on a daring raid to free the prisoners. So much has been written of Andersonville but still the death rate was only 24% where at Point Lookout it was 27%. Federal prisons such as Rock Island had 28% and Elmira, N.Y. had an incredible 44% death rate and while the Confederates held more prisoners, the overall death rate was only 8.36% as opposed to 12.02% in Federal prisons. The bitterness in Southern Maryland was the refusal to allow medicine and warm clothing into Point Lookout and the refusal of Federal authorities to send medicine or supplies to their own people at Andersonville.

Although General Butler agreed to an exchange of prisoners who were sick and dying, General Grant refused to honor the agreement. The most brutal of the blacks were made guards and competed in the shooting of prisoners which went unpunished. The Provost Marshall made more than $1,000,000 from his position at camp. Without blankets or bedding it was usual to find four to seven prisoners frozen to death in the morning and by 1865 the death rate was 60 to 65 a day.

So devastating was the morale in Southern Maryland by Point Lookout, which held mostly prisoners from North Carolina, that General Lee decided on a daring plan to free them. It was all the more daring because General Grant was at that moment threatening Richmond with tremendous forces. The task was given to General Early in July of 1864 to be assisted by Maryland's General Johnson. The plan was to cross the Potomac north of Washington. Early was to attack Washington sending the Union ships scurrying from Point Lookout. General Johnson was to proceed from Washington to Baltimore severing communications and destroying bridges. This he did successfully even stopping to burn Maryland Governor Bradford's home. An attack from the Potomac by ships was to complete the mission. In the meantime every Southern Maryland home and northern Virginia home had been contacted to take and hide and care for those too ill to travel. All went well. General Early's attack on Fort Stevens was so successful, had he known he could have taken Washington. General Johnson had succeeded with his mission and was headed for Point Lookout from Baltimore when two things happened—supplies failed to arrive in time for the attack from the Potomac and the Union got word of the plan. General Lee was forced to call off the operation.

What role Dr. Stone played in the Civil War I can only surmise, but Prince George's County, the largest county in Maryland at one time, and the county from which most of the District of Columbia is carved, gave President Lincoln only one vote. On the adjoining farm to Dr. Stone, Walter Bowie was caught as a spy in the house of T.B. Craycroft and imprisoned at the Capital Prison in Washington where he escaped with the aid of an aunt and a cousin who bribed the prison guard. T.B. Craycroft was himself a "courier" as was every other Southern Marylander. His son was to marry a granddaughter of Dr. Stone.

Dr. Stone himself was fifty-nine at the outbreak of the Civil War, or as Robert Pogue calls it in "Yesteryear in Old St. Mary's County," "The War of the Invasion of the North." Besides being a doctor, as the Examiner of Schools for Prince George's County, he had a legitimate excuse for wide travel.

My mother says Union troops used his barn for quarters. When Dr. Stone complained of abuse of his property the Union leader strung the offender up by his thumbs. Dr. Stone was horrified and went out and cut the man down.

On another occasion on one of his prolonged trips sometimes taking a week or ten days on school business, Union troops came to take his horses. His ten year old son, Tom, went out with a gun and threatened to kill the Union leader if he took them at which the Union leader laughed and decided against it.

Anna Lee once told me Union troops rode their horses into St. Mary's Chapel at the corner of the farm and fed their horses from the baptismal font to show their contempt. But houses and property in Southern Maryland were not burned.

Only a conditioned hatred of Lincoln and "Yankees" in my great-great-aunts and Dr. Stones other descendants, who remembered and recounted atrocities at Point Lookout and retold accounts of relatives and friends in St. Mary's County who were seized and imprisoned, are any indication of family participation in the Secret Service of the Confederacy with the exception of three tell-tale items I found and could only surmise as to why no one ever mentioned their existence.

What President Lincoln had thought to be a "Ninety-day War" escalated and there came a determination in Southerners to take the war they had suffered to Northern soil, to deplete the banks and to do all "but kill or abuse women and children as the Northerners had done." The plan to invade the North from Canada was to draw Union troops from hard hit areas such as the Shenandoah and to seize money to further the war in the Southern cause.

And so during the last year of the Civil War a series of spectacular and daring ventures occurred, for money and supplies were running out.

MAP OF ST. ALBANS' RAID
AND SPY TRAILS TO CANADA

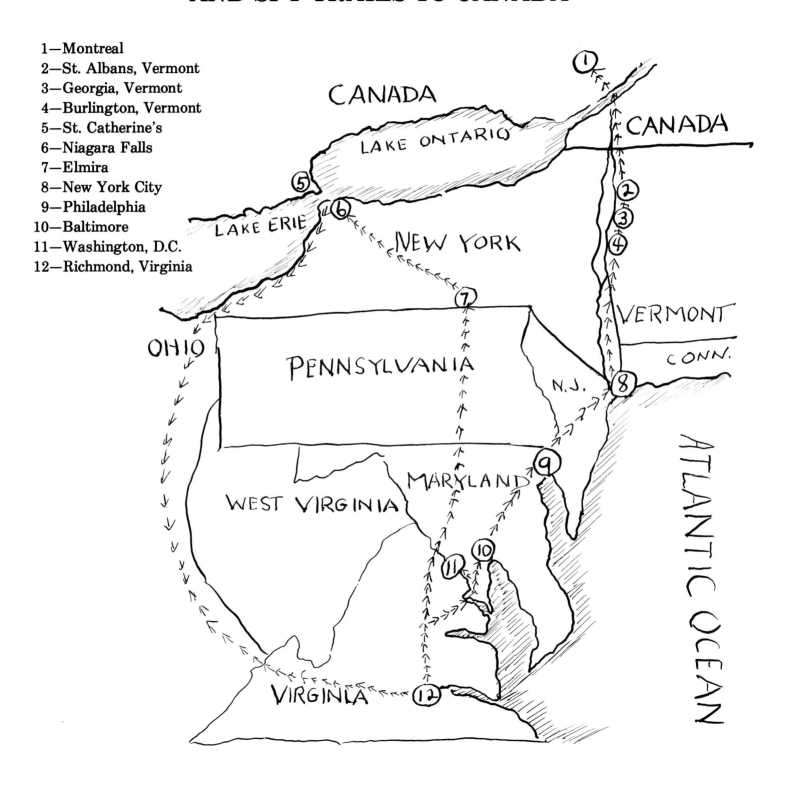

1—Montreal
2—St. Albans, Vermont
3—Georgia, Vermont
4—Burlington, Vermont
5—St. Catherine's
6—Niagara Falls
7—Elmira
8—New York City
9—Philadelphia
10—Baltimore
11—Washington, D.C.
12—Richmond, Virginia

THE CIVIL WAR: REBELS IN CANADA

Several years before the Civil War, Dr. Stone had hired a teacher for his children from St. Mary's Seminary at St. Mary's City. Emily Colton, or "Aunt Nina," as she was known to the family, held school in a room over the slave quarters. Her father, William Colton, had gone from Georgia, Vermont, to King George, Virginia, where he had married Anna Saunders of "Locust Grove," a cousin of James Madison. "Aunt Nina's" brother, Walter Colton, was to marry Dr. Stone's daughter, Mary, five years after the Civil War.

William, one of many children, had brothers and sisters living at St. Albans, Vermont, near the Canadian border as well as Georgia, Vermont, a few miles to the south on Lake Champlain.

In April of 1861, following the firing on Fort Sumpter, Queen Victoria had issued a proclamation recognizing the Confederacy and the Confederacy began seeking ways through Union territory to Canada for the purpose of ordering supplies from England and by-passing the Union blockade. Commissioners were sent to Montreal.

In mid-May of 1861. Abigail Colton, from Georgia, Vermont, first cousin of "Aunt Nina," wrote her sister, Mary, an obviously coded letter to Stewartsville, Virginia. Her sister was married to a Canadian doctor who, after the war, was to live in St. Albans. The letter was apparently in reply to a letter received hidden in a dress sleeve. Apologizing for not having written sooner, Abigail wrote, "the fact is owing to the times I hadn't much faith you would receive it if I did write and thought it went into the dead letter office for old Abe's private purposes. I did not care to waste my 'ammunition.' " She then invites them up for the summer, takes pot-shots at some friends and relatives underlined, and makes happy chit-chatty remarks about others, also underlined. This, I believe, was intended to indicate who could be trusted to be Confederate sympathizers and who could not. At the end, she again invites them up indicating that at her house the coast would be clear.

I believe this was a first step in setting up one of the spy trails for the Confederacy to Canada. Three and one half years later, Abigail's cousins by marriage, George Sanders and his son Lewis Sanders, were to be among the architects of the famous Confederate raid on three banks in St. Albans, Vermont, conducted from Canada. After the war, George Sanders' financial records were brought down from Canada to Washington to the trial of the Lincoln assassination conspirators in an attempt to prove that John Wilkes Booth had been on his payroll. It was he who was to serve the longest exile of any Confederate following the Civil War for his role in the St. Albans' Raid and other activities.

George Sanders, from Kentucky was sent early to Canada as a commissioner. At one time he had ordered six iron-clads from England but for some unknown reason these never materialized. His family was originally from Spotsylvania, Virginia, and, although he spelled his name without the "U," he was a cousin of Anna Saunders, "Aunt Nina's" mother.

A curious connection with my father occurred two years ago. George Sanders' wife was a daughter of Samuel Chester Reid, a naval hero of the War of 1812. During the 1930s my father commissioned and commanded the destroyer Reid, named for that great sailor-warrior. The Reid was to have a fine record in

World War II until she was finally sunk toward the end of the war. Two years ago my father gave the commissioning address for the new Samuel Chester Reid in California. The ship had been christened by a direct descendent of Samuel Reid and George Sanders.

Chester Reid was to design the American flag in the format that it exists today. In 1816 Congress authorized Captain Reid to redesign the American flag which had become too unwieldy with 15 stripes. Changing the stripes from states for stripes to stripes for the original 13 colonies, he arranged the field of a star for each state to be placed in parallel rows. In 1818, Reid's flag with 13 stripes and twenty stars flew over the U.S. House of Representatives.

In Walter Colton's small box of treasures in the attic, I found, along with *Three Years in California* and the miniature of Walter Colton, the Chaplain, a treatise called "A Bible View of Slavery" by John Henry Hopkins, the Bishop of Vermont, published in 1863 in London by Otley and Saunders and justifying slavery. I was surprised and curious because I knew the name of Saunders to be the maiden name of Walter Colton's mother, and I was curious that the Bishop of Vermont would have Southern sympathies, and I also knew Walter Colton's father had come from Vermont.

Bishop Hopkins' treatise was to create a furor in newspapers in New England during the Civil War and afterwards there was an attempt made to have the clergy who had voiced sympathies for the South to be hanged as traitors. This was not successful.

Bishop Hopkins had been raised in Frederick, Maryland, a "Southern" town, but now lived in Burlington, Vermont.

It is probable that the Saunders who published this treatise was also a relative of Walter Colton.

Curiosity over the coincidence of the Saunders name and why a Vermont Bishop would have Southern sympathies combined with the fact that I knew Walter Colton's father had come from Vermont, sent me sleuthing again. It was from this treatise that I was to unravel a tale of Civil War intrigue that was to apparently involve many members of my family.

By mid-1863, the Confederacy had suffered severe setbacks and was financially depleted. Bold and innovative plans were being formed. Early in May of 1864, Jefferson Davis sent Jacob Thompson, former Secretary of Interior in Buchanan's administration and Clement Clay, a former Congressman from Mississippi, to Canada as Commissioners. Thompson deposited three quarters of a million dollars in the bank of Montreal and set up his headquarters at Toronto while Clay made his at St. Catherine's near Niagara. This was for the purpose of staging raids on the North from the Canadian border.

It was George Sanders (now an ex-officio commissioner) who behind the scenes was to dream up an incredible plan that was to fail and another that was to be a whopping success.

The first was to create an uprising in Illinois, Indiana, and Ohio with 175,000 supporters in those states, to seize Chicago, enlist the support of the delegates of the National Democratic Convention, free prisoners at Camp Douglass and with the help of escaped prisoners, Confederate refugees, and Union Deserters all living in Canada, to take over Kentucky and Missouri. One of the leaders to seize Chicago was

John Castleman, a nephew of Vice-President John Breckinridge in President Buchanan's administration. (Breckinridge had become a general in the Confederate Army.) The plan was foiled by an informer and Castleman was sentenced to death. At the last minute, President Lincoln commuted the death sentence in an act of compassion on a plea from another Breckinridge uncle, loyal to the Union.

Bennett Young from Kentucky, had been one of the 2,500 of Morgan's Raiders who had been captured in the summer of '63 in Ohio, but had escaped to Canada from Camp Douglass. He had relatives from Maryland, the most notable probably having been Richard Bennett, the Puritan leader of the overthrow of the Maryland Government during the Cromwellian period.

Bennett devised a plan approved by Clay and Jefferson Davis, to raid a series of Vermont towns beginning with St. Albans. The purpose was to bring the war to the North, hopefully to divert Union troops from such hard hit areas as the Shenandoah and by robbing banks to help the financially depleted South.

In August, Bennett had gone to Chicago to join in the plot to seize that city. There he recruited 20 Confederate soldiers who had escaped from Federal prisons, for the purpose of carrying out raids on the border. Most of these young men, hardly more than twenty-one, were from Kentucky and veterans of Morgan's Raiders. They were sons or nephews of ministers, congressmen, and senators.

Bennett arrived in St. Albans, Vermont, with two raiders on October 15th. He obtained lodging at the Tremont Hotel while his two companions checked in at the American House. For the next few days he was seen around the village chatting with shop keepers and several times on the village green with an unidentified young lady in deep religious discussion. (Bennett Young was now a theological student in Canada.)

On the 19th, several raiders came in by buggy from Burlington where Bishop John Henry Hopkins resided.

On October 19th some twenty-one raiders were ready for their mission. Bennett Young took six or seven of the raiders to patrol the village green and divided the rest into three groups.

At exactly 3:00, Thomas Collins and four others entered the Bank of St. Albans and at the same moment another group entered the Franklin County Bank while the third group entered the First National Bank.

Thomas Collins, son of a Baptist minister seized the teller. "What does all this mean?" he was asked. "We are confederate soldiers . . . come North to rob and plunder; the same as you did in the Shenandoah Valley and in other parts of the South." Collins then proceeded to administer the oath of allegiance to the Confederate States of America to the five terrified prisoners. They were told to swear to uphold the Confederacy and its beloved President, Jefferson Davis.

At the First National Bank, Caleb Wallace, nephew of a Kentucky Senator, told his prisoners he represented the Confederate States of America. "We have come to retaliate for acts committed against our people by General Sherman." At the Franklin County Bank the raider Huntley told his captives they had come to rob the banks and burn the town in retaliation for what had been committed by Union troops in the South.

ST. ALBANS' RAIDERS AND PLOTTERS

Four of the young men pictured are Confederate soldiers who participated in the St. Albans' Raid, the Reverend Cameron had been a courier between Canada and Richmond during the Civil War and his appearance in the picture was probably in the role as one of the architects of the operation. Saunders is listed as an assistant to Clay, the Confederate Commissioner. It is probable he was Lewis Sanders, George's son, who handled the finances of the "Raiders" and secured their defense attorneys.

Bennett Young, the leader of the "Raiders," was to become a highly respected citizen of Kentucky and eventually the head of 40,000 Confederate veterans.

Rev. Cameron   Scott   Teavis

Hutchinson   Saunders   Bennett Young
(alias Huntley)

Courtesy of the St. Albans' Historical Society

On taking money from a customer, one raider was asked if he had no respect for private property to which the raider replied, "Grant, Sherman and Sheridan do not respect private property and neither do we."

Grabbing horses stolen from a local livery stable and with $223,800 in bank notes, currency, and bonds and seizing horses on the street, the raiders took off for Canada leaving one dead and one seriously wounded, slinging bottles of "Greek fire" against the building walls as they dashed for the border.

That the raiders had friends in the area was attested to by one mortally wounded raider who was hidden and cared for on a farm a short distance from St. Albans until a Canadian secretly took him to Montreal where he died. Other wounded raiders were cared for by a Canadian doctor sympathetic to the South.

On arriving in Canada they scattered and went in different directions. Elated by their success and confident of their protection of the Canadian government they showed little concern when fourteen of the twenty-one were arrested and taken into custody by the Canadian government. The seven who escaped presumably took their booty back to the Confederate government while fifty thousand dollars was confiscated temporarily from the fourteen prisoners by the Canadian government. But in the Montreal jail, wine flowed, meals were lavish, and the raiders were openly cheered by Canadians in the streets and even in court. Bennett Young immediately wrote a letter to Canadian newspapers to explain the raid as retaliation for the brutal treatment of Union troops of towns, property and people and the robbing of banks in the south. Like a little boy thumbing his nose in victory he wrote the newspaper "Messenger" in St. Albans thanking the young lady who walked with him on the village green several times for inspiring him to victory and requesting a subscription to the newspaper to be sent to a hotel as he expected to be released soon. He graciously released raid victims from their oath of allegiance to the Confederacy.

Of the young lady he wrote, "Tell her I am deeply indebted to her for her soothing influence which the music of her siren voice had upon me on the dawning of that memorable day when she sang to me the words of that beautiful and affecting song, 'Oh Just Before the Battle, Mother.' It assuredly gave me the great encouragement for the work before us, and no doubt enabled me in great measure to exercise my part of it successfully." If the young lady sang such a song, surely she knew what was coming!

The Commissioners hired all the best lawyers in Canada leaving the leftovers for the Union lawyers filing for extradition. Lawyers for the St. Albans' Banks were hardly equal to these men, particularly the brilliant John Abbott, who was later to become Prime Minister of Canada. With the Union fighting desperately for extradition, the bank lawyers were trying to establish the raiders as common robbers and murderers for as such, extradition was possible, but Abbott successfully established the raid as an act of war under orders and thereby entitled to the sanctuary of a "neutral" country.

The Saunders shown in the photograph as assistant to Clay was probably Lewis Sanders, son of George Sanders, who handled all of the financing of the "Raiders" and the attorneys for the defense. It is probable that both he and his father were among the architects of the St. Albans' Raid.

The Reverend Cameron apparently was involved in the plot although not listed as a raider. He had been a courier to Richmond using the Church and the "cloth" as he went. At a later time, when he was to go to Richmond to secure copies of commissions and orders from Jefferson Davis, he returned through the tight security of Union territory disguised as a Catholic priest accompanied by two nuns. After the Civil War, he was to marry the daughter of a Confederate general who lived not far from Bel Air, Maryland, the home of John Wilkes Booth.

When the judge finally rendered his decision that the Raiders had indeed behaved in an act of war and were free to go, spectators in the court room and in the streets cheered wildly.

The "Raiders" strode from the room, picked up the $50,000 awaiting in the back of the court house room from a Canadian agent, leaped into sleighs piled high with furs and fled into oblivion. The Union was furious, called the waiting money and sleighs fore knowledge of the judge's decision and called the procedure high-handed—even threatening retaliatory attacks on Canada. Canadian officials became alarmed at a serious rift with the Union and set out to re-arrest the "Raiders" for a new hearing under a different judge. Four had set out for Halifax not arriving until the end of April in 1865 after enduring a severe winter and many hardships, where they learned the war had ended and the President had been assassinated. Tearfully they took a boat for England where they spent a few years in exile.

Christmas Eve, in 1864, five raiders were caught in New Hampshire where cold and hunger had driven them to enlist in the Union army. Here they hoped to be sent to combat where they could jump across the lines to the Confederate side. When they were identified, they bribed their captor with $700 to allow them to escape.

Bennett Young, with Huntley and Teavis travelled 300 miles to St. Francis in snow and bitter cold where they walked right into the arms of the Canadian law. When they arrived back at the Montreal Jail they found two other raiders had been captured.

The hearing proceeded much as before but it became evident that affidavits from Jefferson Davis in Richmond verifying Confederate commissions would be needed to prove that the raid had been carried out under specific orders. Lt. Davis, a Confederate refugee in Canada, was sent on the mission but was captured in Ohio and sentenced to death as a spy. Three days before his execution, President Lincoln commuted his sentence.

Then it is probable that several couriers were sent to Richmond, but two are positively known: One, Sara Slater from North Carolina had been sent to Canada early in the war because of her ability with the French language (she had been escorted several times to Richmond by John Surratt and his mother). The other was the Reverend Cameron.

While the two couriers were en route to Richmond the trial continued. Thomas Stone, one of Morgan's Raiders, testified he had known all five of the prisoners, that he had seen a copy of Bennett Young's orders and he had himself originally planned to join them. Thomas Stone was Dr. Stone's nephew by his oldest brother, William.

"Rose Hill" at Port Tobacco, was one of the last places on the spy trail to Canada before crossing the Potomac into Confederate territory.

Olivia Floyd at "Rose Hill" received one dispatch to Richmond to secure commissions and orders from

"ROSE HILL"—1745
Port Tobacco, Maryland

"Rose Hill" was built by Dr. Gustavus Brown, George Washington's doctor, who was with him when he died. His sister was married to Thomas Stone, the Signer, and it was his father who purchased Lord Somerville.

During the Civil War, it was one of the last spots on the spy trail from Canada to Richmond before crossing the Potomac into the Confederate States. The owner at that time was Olivia Floyd, a cousin of Admiral Raphael Semmes (her mother was a Semmes). Receiving messages from Canada, she would place them in the crotch of a tree on the bank of Port Tobacco Creek where they were picked up and taken to Richmond.

Jefferson Davis, placing it in an andiron seconds before Union troops arrived. One officer put his heel upon the andiron while he questioned her. After their departure she tucked the paper in her hair and took it to the river bank and placed it in the crotch of a tree where it was picked up and taken to Richmond. Forty years later at the great Louisville Confederate celebration she presented Bennett Young with a wooden boat in which she had also hidden messages.

Both Sara Slater and Stephen Cameron arrived back the same day, Sara Slater with affidavits, and the Reverend Cameron with copies.

Thus the trial ended setting the "Raiders" free on extradition charges. But Union and bank attorneys were only mollified when it was learned that the prisoners would be tried for the violation of "neutrality" laws there being some doubt as to whether the plot had been hatched on Canadian soil.

On April 6, 1865, new charges were made, but only one poor witness of questionable character appeared for the prosecution. As a result, all of the "Raiders" were allowed to go free except for Bennett Young. Three days after the new charges were made, General Lee was to surrender.

Benett Young, in testifying at his second trial for extradition, which if it succeeded would have meant certain death, stated, "my heart is opposed, as most others, to measures of retaliation but . . . fresh from the scenes of devastated firesides and ruined villages, and listening so lately to the wail of the widow and the cry of the orphan . . . having espoused that cause I will never look back, but rather than yield, I will pour out my blood as a sacrifice at the altar of the noblest cause that can call forth the efforts of man.

"I have faced death many times ere this; and should I, contrary to all precedent, be extradited, I am perfectly well aware what my fate shall be. I can die as a son of the South."

Months before, John Wilkes Booth had written in his diary as he fled south toward certain death, "I hoped for no gain, I knew no private wrong. I struck for my country and her alone. A people ground beneath this tyranny prayed for this end."

A few days later as he lay dying on the Garrett porch, among his last words he said, "Tell Mother I died for my country." Who is to say who is a hero and who is a villain in war? For although both were apparently part of the same section of the Secret Service of the Confederacy, Bennett Young was to emerge a great hero and the name of Booth has gone down in history in infamy.

The St. Albans' Raid was hailed as a great victory for the South—achieving its full mission—to draw Union troops north and gain badly needed money. The raid struck terror into the towns and cities on the Canadian border from Maine to Michigan. In Vermont, it was believed that this was just the advanced guard of an invading army from Canada.

At Burlington, Vermont, fear took over. It was rumored that ships had been captured on Lake Champlain and a wide-scale invasion was under way from Canada. Terrorized Cleveland daily expected attack by armored ships from across the lake. Buffalo awaited an attack on the day of the General Election. Every man able to fight was called out. In December, a Senator from Michigan told his fellow senators, "We have been under a continual state of alarm for fear of incendiaries, murders, and robbers from the

Canadian frontier." And on into February, rumors circulated in New York that raiders were organized in Canada to attack New York cities.

The great scare on the northern frontier had indeed drawn a large number of Union troops from the South to defend the Canadian border, but it was too late and not enough.

The following October, long after the war was over, the charges were dropped against Bennett Young for lack of evidence and witnesses.

Going to London, he joined Vice-President Breckinridge in exile, with whom he lived for several years studying law—but not before he married a Kentucky sweetheart at Niagara Falls. On returning to Kentucky, he became a great citizen, president of railroads, attorney to governors, and author of many books. He had the most comprehensive archaeological library in his time, and he became the head of 40,000 Confederate veterans. He was as loyal to his country and the Union as he had been in his devotion to the Confederacy. But for all his prolific writing, he never did write one word of the St. Albans' Raid. One can only surmise that in integrity, he protected the identity of the other participants to his grave, but back in Kentucky, the "Raiders" met frequently and loved telling the story of their wild adventure.

In 1905, a huge celebration was held in Louisville, Kentucky. Bennett Young, in a spanking new Confederate uniform led the parade with his "Raiders." Olivia Floyd was there and presented Bennett with a wooden boat in which she had also hidden messages. Also there was the widow of Stonewall Jackson.

A fifty year celebration of the "Raiders" in Canada was attended by citizens from St. Albans, but even then Bennett refused to discuss the Raid, dismissing it as a wild prank of youth.

President Johnson granted amnesty to almost all Confederate leaders but the handful of St. Albans' Raiders and plotters—perhaps as few as five or six were excluded from his forgiveness.

George Sanders spent the longest exile—11 years—for his role as the power behind the Canadian-based operations.

That same fall the Confederates held Frederick, Maryland, hostage under General Early. They emptied all the banks, undoubtedly with inside help, for Frederick was a "Southern town," the home of Chief Justice Taney, and where the Bishop Hopkins was raised.

And "Nina" Colton's cousins, George Sanders, the commander of Confederate activities in Canada, his son, Lewis, and Saunders, the publisher of the "Bible View of Slavery" surely had a role in a spy trail to Canada and the "St. Albans' Raid," as did her cousin Abigail Colton.

John Wilkes Booth

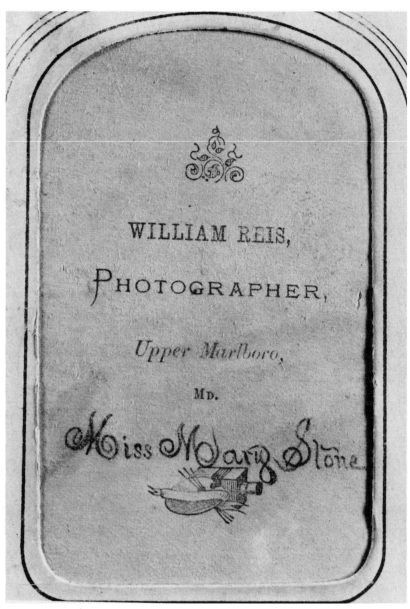

Back of Booth Photograph

The photograph of John Wilkes Booth had the place of honor on the first page of Mary Stone's photograph album. Taken by an Upper Marlboro photographer, on the back is pencilled "Miss Mary Stone."

JOHN H. SURRATT.

Entered according to Act of Congress by John H. Surratt, in the year 1868, in the Clerk's Office of the District Court of the District of Columbia.

David Herold   *John H. Surratt*

On the second page of Mary's album is David Herold who was with Booth on his flight. Apparently, Mary had pencilled in a moustache to make him appear more dashing. John Surratt's picture was made several years after the war and his acquittal when he found himself destitute and sold this one as a souvenir.

SOUTHERN MARYLAND IN
THE CIVIL WAR AND BOOTH'S FLIGHT

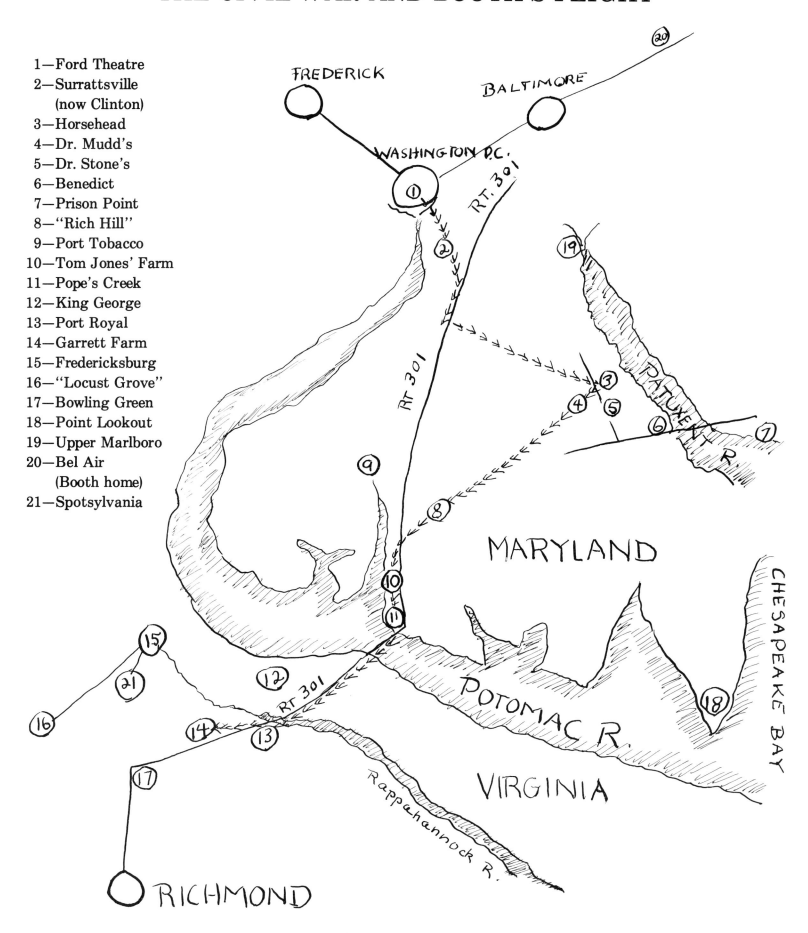

1—Ford Theatre
2—Surrattsville
  (now Clinton)
3—Horsehead
4—Dr. Mudd's
5—Dr. Stone's
6—Benedict
7—Prison Point
8—"Rich Hill"
9—Port Tobacco
10—Tom Jones' Farm
11—Pope's Creek
12—King George
13—Port Royal
14—Garrett Farm
15—Fredericksburg
16—"Locust Grove"
17—Bowling Green
18—Point Lookout
19—Upper Marlboro
20—Bel Air
  (Booth home)
21—Spotsylvania

THE CIVIL WAR: SOUTHERN MARYLAND AND JOHN WILKES BOOTH

In Anna Lee's safe deposit box I found lockets and other jewelry including an unworn, unscratched gold bracelet. Inscribed inside was "Amo te," Te Amo being Latin for "I Love You." The bracelet appeared to be a gift of returned love. But no one in the family knew to whom the bracelet belonged nor from whom it had been given much less why it had never been worn. Yet all of the lockets and other jewelry had been identified.

After two years of sifting through family treasures I finally came to my great-grandmother, Mary Stone's, photograph album. Thumbing through the book trying to identify family members I was startled to find myself looking on the fifth page at the picture of a young man under which was printed as part of the photograph, John H. Surratt, the son of Mrs. Surratt who was hanged for the Lincoln assassination plot. Going back to the first picture I was flabbergasted to recognize John Wilkes Booth. Taken by an Upper Marlboro photographer, on the back with flourishing capitals in pencil was printed, Miss Mary Stone. She was by the fall of '64, eighteen years old.

On the second page was a picture of young David Herold who was with Booth during his 10 day flight. Apparently Mary had pencilled in a moustache to make him look older and more dashing.

It was these three photographs that put me on the trail of learning more of the Civil War, for I could not understand how this could possibly have happened. How could these three villains, as I had been taught to believe, be in my great-grandmother's book with John Wilkes Booth on the first page, in the place of honor.

As the Fall of '64 approached there were new developments in the Secret Service of the Confederacy. Mrs. Surratt who had been widowed two years before, left her farmhouse at Surrattsville (now known as Clinton) in Southern Maryland, for the struggle to run the farm badly stripped by Union troops was beyond her. Moving to a house owned by the Surratt family on "H" Street in Washington and converting it to a rooming house, the house in Clinton was rented as a tavern.

Two years before, Anna Surratt, Mrs. Surratt's daughter, had written a remote cousin of Dr. Stone's, Louise Stone, with whom she had gone to school. Describing the death of her father, she said "and all of this was happening while the *man from across the Potomac was visiting us.*"

It was in the fall then that the actor, John Wilkes Booth, became friends with John Surratt in the Secret Service of the Confederacy and along with other agents frequented the house on "H" Street. And it was in the fall of '64 that John Wilkes Booth was in Southern Maryland spending a night with Dr. Mudd in a plot to abduct President Lincoln and take him to Richmond.

Early Monday morning, April 10, 1865, word reached Washington that General Lee had surrendered. A week before Walter Colton had been wounded and taken prisoner at Richmond. But all of Lee's generals had still not surrendered. Between Monday and Friday the plot was hatched to wipe out Lincoln, Grant, Johnson, and Seward. The conspirators would go south and join the generals who had not yet surrendered, the fight would go on and the South would win.

Mrs. Lincoln's sympathies were known to be for the South, for she had three brothers who had died fighting for the Confederacy. She had been known to call General Grant a "butcher" in public and once

"ELLERSLIE"—1745
Port Tobacco, Maryland

Built by Dr. Stone's great-grandparents, Elizabeth Hanson (sister of John Hanson) and Dr. Daniel Jenifer, it was originally called Coates Retirement. After the Civil War the owners went to Kentucky to the home of Mary Todd Lincoln, named "Ellerslie" for the place in Scotland from which the Todd family had come. On their return they changed the name of their plantation from Coates Retirement to "Ellerslie" which was rather remarkable since Charles County had given Mary Lincoln's husband only one vote in his 1860 election.

Maryland records show ten Todd marriages dating back to 1710, most of which are recorded at St. Margaret's Parish near Annapolis. The dates suggest the Todds were Jacobite exiles and it is probable Mary Todd Lincoln had many relatives in Southern Maryland.

B. Taussig '83

during the Civil War, President Lincoln was forced to testify before Congress that his wife was not supplying the Confederacy with information. She had Todd relatives in Maryland. History has been so unkind to her but I see her as a tragic figure caught in a devastating situation. And my sympathy is with poor President Lincoln who inherited a pre-designed course, and whose only motive was to preserve the Union which was so necessary.

Small wonder that after that Friday the 14th, on the fateful night at the Ford Theatre, Mrs. Lincoln was to lose her mind.

The agents of the Confederate Secret Service had precise information as to the whereabouts of cabinet members at a given time Friday night, April 14th. It is difficult for me to believe that Mrs. Lincoln did not help a cause she so deeply espoused but if she did insist on her husband attending the theatre that night, and as some insinuated at the urging of others, there is also no doubt in my mind that she knew not for what purpose. It is said she cried out, "And I brought him here for this!"

But early in the morning towards the last of his waning life when she was finally allowed in the room with him she cradled his head in her arms sobbing incoherently and fought with every ounce of her those who would drag her from his bedside. She loved her husband.

Early Friday afternoon John Wilkes Booth had gone to Mrs. Surratt's boarding house on "H" Street. There he had given her a package of guns, ammunition and a spy glass and asked her to take it to Surrattsville to the Surratt farmhouse converted into a tavern.

Booth, a successful actor, a dashing lady's man, was very much a part of the social scene in Washington. If not an aristocrat, the doors of the socially elite were open to him in the nation's capital. Engaged to Bessie Hale, the daughter of the Senator from New Hampshire, the possible consequences of the act he committed was not a deterrent as a threat to the end of his personal happiness or welfare, for his devotion to his cause was a total commitment. It deeply distressed him only that his actions would surely cause severe unknown punishment to his own family and particularly to his mother.

As Booth sped toward the 11th Street bridge by the Navy Yard, Lewis Paine of Virginia, a former Confederate soldier, was leaving the Seward house where he had just made an unsuccessful attempt on the life of the Secretary of State. After entering the bedroom of the ailing secretary his gun failed to fire. Using a knife he lashed out at the horrified victim who managed to roll out of bed and attract household members. Although sustaining cuts he avoided serious injury.

Also marked for death was General Grant, but because he was on a train to New Jersy, he was spared. Vice President Johnson was assigned to George Atzerodt, a carriage maker from Port Tobacco. Although he went to Johnson's hotel, it is not quite clear why he never made the attempt.

On arriving at Surrattsville, Booth picked up his package of guns and ammunition and joined David Herold, a clerk from Port Tobacco. By then his broken leg had become excruciatingly painful and he was forced to take a detour from his destination to Pope's Creek where a boat had been hidden in the rushes.

He changed his course and he and David Herold set out for Dr. Mudd's. Our family lore says that at Horsehead he asked at the tavern for the nearest doctor. Dr. Mudd was four miles on the right fork and Dr.

Stone was six miles on the left fork. It had always been a family joke, "but for two miles our names would have been Mudd." I don't think any of us knew how nearly right we might have been. The fall before, records show Booth had spent the night at the Horsehead tavern, as well as having spent a night at Dr. Mudd's.

Dr. Mudd cut away his painful boot, put splints on his leg and gave him crutches. By now it was nearly dawn and Dr. Mudd gave him a bed—the same bed he had slept in the fall before while the plot to abduct Lincoln was hatched in Southern Maryland.

In the morning David Herold and Dr. Mudd went to Bryantown where they found Federal troops everywhere. David returned alone to the Mudd house, and he and Booth gathered themselves for a quick departure through the swamps to "Rich Hill." Certainly Dr. Mudd knew by this time what Booth had done and surely he knew who he was. That Dr. Mudd gave Booth the opportunity to escape is probable and it is exactly what every Southern Marylander to a man would have done, and everyone who had the opportunity did do.

So the two set out for the home of Colonel Samuel Cox of "Rich Hill." Oddly enough it was this same plantation where Lord Somerville had been indentured nearly 150 years before.

Samuel Cox, very active in the Secret Service of the Confederacy had spent some months in the Capital Prison in Washington the first year of the war. As the storm clouds had gathered he had collected a large arsenal of guns and ammunition for Charles County, which was confiscated by the Union, even before war was declared.

On Monday afternoon Federal troops arrived at Mrs. Surratt's house in Washington. While they were there a man appeared at the door professing to have come to do yard work for Mrs. Surratt. Investigation proved him to be Lewis Paine and he and Mrs. Surratt were arrested.

Late Saturday night Booth and Herold arrived at Cox's house where they were given blankets and food and hidden in a grove of trees a mile to the south.

The following morning Thomas Jones appeared to give help and to prepare for a crossing into Virginia. Jones, as a postmaster had acted as a courier for messages to and from Richmond. This was a daily affair from Washington. (Dr. Stoughton Dent made almost daily trips to Pope's Creek also.) In addition, Jones had been arrested for transporting many people by boat to Virginia. For this he had spent some months in the Captial Prison the first year of the war. On his release he had agreed to continue his operation but only if all agents were under his command. For the rest of the war he successfully transported messages and people across the Potomac, cleverly outmaneuvering Union gunboats. For five days Jones brought newspapers and food and arranged for David to take the horses into the swamp and shoot them lest their identity betray them.

Booth had an 1864 Diary from which he had written a note to Cox, bitter that although he had been given food, blankets, and a place to hide that he had not been taken into the Cox home for he felt he had committed an act of heroism for which all Confederate patriots should be grateful. I believe they were, but Cox feared for his family.

During his five days in the woods near "Rich Hill" Booth took out his diary and turning to an empty page at the top of which was written "te Amo," suggesting perhaps that the diary had been given to him by a young lady, he wrote ". . . for six months we worked to capture . . . but our cause being almost lost, something decisive and great must be done . . ." In saying the cause was almost lost he still believed it was not over.

I could not help wondering if Mary Stone had given Booth the diary in which was written "te Amo" and if he had given her the bracelet inscribed "Amo te." Did he by writing on that page hope it would find its way back to Dr. Stone and Mary for Dr. Stone had been born not 2 miles from "Rich Hill" at "Equality." With many empty pages in the diary why did he choose that one? I shall never know. That he had the place of honor on the first page of her photograph album and that she knew him there could be no doubt, and there could be no doubt that he was special to her.

Thursday night Jones came for Booth and Herold bringing a horse for Booth. Taking them to a barn near his own farm he brought them food and then they set out and crossing Dent's meadow, started across the Potomac. Not far from shore Jones spotted a gunboat and they scurried back to shore pulling the boat into the underbrush and hiding Booth nearby. Herold and Jones scampered up the cliff. Two crew members walked a few feet away from Booth without detecting him.

On Friday Jones appeared to tell them that they could have his boat and he would give them names of people and directions to farms where they would be helped and be safe, but that his house was being watched and it would be too risky for him to take them. However, the rumor had been spread that Booth had been seen in St. Mary's County and Federal troops had been diverted making it safe to leave that night.

On this day Friday, the 21st, he wrote in his diary, "After being hunted like a dog through swamps and woods, and last night being chased by gunboats til I was forced to return, wet, cold, and starving, with every man's hand against me, I am here in despair . . . I hoped for no gain; I knew no private wrong. I struck for my country and her alone. A people ground beneath this tyranny prayed for this end, and yet now see the cold hands they extend me . . . I have too great a soul to die like a criminal. Oh! May he spare me that, let me die bravely . . . And for this brave boy, Herold, here with me, who often prays (yes, before and since) with a true and sincere heart, was it a crime in him?"

That night they set out and after rowing for sometime put into a cove. In the morning they discovered they were still on the Maryland side. Herold went up to the plantation of his old friend Colonel Hughes and brought back the perennial Maryland ham and newspapers. Booth then learned of the capture of Atzerodt, and that there was a $50,000 reward for him and $25,000 each for John Surratt and David Herold.

The following night they successfully crossed the Potomac and on Sunday threaded their way through trusted contacts toward Port Royal. Stopping on the way Sunday night at the home of Dr. Stewart who fed them and examined Booth's painful leg and put him up for the night a short distance away in the cabin of a negro freedman. Booth again showed his bitterness at not being taken into the protection of the homes of those involved in the Confederate Secret Service. In another note to Dr. Stewart he wrote, ". . . I hate to blame you for want of hospitality . . . I was sick, tired with a broken leg . . . I would not have turned a dog from my door in such a condition. However you were kind enough to give us something to eat . . . but on account of the reluctant manner in which it was bestowed I feel bound to pay for it."

On Monday, the 24th, at Port Conway they ran into three of Mosby's men having been disbanded, on their way south to join General Johnson who still had not surrendered. The three Confederate soldiers took Booth and Herold to the Garrett farm about three miles beyond Port Royal. The following day David Herold went to Bowling Green with the three Confederate soldiers to buy himself some shoes. In the afternoon he returned with two of the soldiers, the third having stayed in Bowling Green to visit his girl.

In the meantime a special detachment of 25 Union soldiers had been assigned to scour the Virginia side of the Potomac looking for the two fugitives. At Port Royal the ferryman finally revealed that Booth and Herold had passed that way in the company of three Confederate soldiers going to Bowling Green.

The two Confederate soldiers rode back to Port Royal, probably on a scouting trip, and not long after returned breathlessly to warn their friends the Federal troops were on the way.

Passing the Garrett farm the troops rode on to Bowling Green where they found the third Confederate soldier, and under the threat of death for concealing the whereabouts of Booth he finally made it known that he was hiding at the Garrett farm.

David Herold was allowed to surrender and Booth was removed from the burning barn having been shot in the head, whether by his own hand or by a Federal troop was never determined. Not long after, he slipped away on the porch of the Garrett farm house.

In July, Mrs. Surratt, George Atzerodt, David Herold, and John Paine were hanged. Mrs. Surratt arrived in black supported by two priests, the soldier Paine strode proudly and arrogantly to his death. Snatching a hat from an officer and placing it on his own head he marched to his death.

Strangely the four had been convicted by court martial and a military commission with charges that included Jefferson Davis and testimony of outrages committed by Confederate troops.

George Sanders records were brought down from Canada in an effort to establish that he had financed John Wilkes Booth.

Of the four charged with conspiracy to assassinate the President, one is considered by many to have been innocent. That Mrs. Surratt was in the Secret Service of the Confederacy there is no doubt and might have been hanged as a spy; but this was not what she was charged with. Whether she really knew what was in the package she took to Surrattsville or why she was taking it there has never been established. George Calvert, direct descendent of the Maryland proprietary family testified on her behalf that she had made the trip to Surrattsville to discuss finances with Lloyd who had rented the Surratt farm house for a tavern in which George Calvert had money invested and that she had only incidentally carried the package. Lewis Paine professed her innocence of the plot until he was hanged which he did not do for himself or the other two convicted. It is doubtful that she was involved or had knowledge of the plot itself, but was only in the continuing role of support of Southern interests.

Dr. Stone's nephew Frederick Stone, from Port Tobacco, was counsel to David Herold and said sadly she was convicted "for lack of evidence." People in Southern Maryland to this day defend her vehemently and there are many today who would try to clear her name even as the name of Samuel Mudd has recently been cleared, that although engaged in the Secret Service of the Confederacy she was not specifically involved in the plot.

Mrs. Surratt's son, John Surratt, escaped to Canada from whence he went to Egypt. Several years later he was extradited from Italy and was tried and acquitted. His name appears as registered at a hotel in Elmira, New York, that fateful night. But there is a curious thing that happened; his handkerchief, embroidered with J.H. Surratt was picked up in the railway station at St. Albans, Vermont, soon after the assassination. Federal agents went there looking for him and it is probable it was deliberately dropped there by friends to throw pursuers off his trail. The spy trail to Canada through St. Albans being nearly twice the distance of that from Elmira to Canada, it is more probable he went the shorter route.

That there were other assassination plots in the wind is evident. How many people were involved in the Booth plot has never been determined. Certainly some of the employees at the Ford theatre were involved and telegraph wires from Washington were out of commission for two hours that night of the assassination.

Vice President Johnson was a Southerner, not popular with many in the Union administration. During the testimony of his impeachment trial after he became president, he was accused of complicity in the Lincoln plot and it was charged that he had the most to gain by its success. These charges were dropped. He was a newly elected Vice President having been the military governor of Tennessee and probably having been chosen with the hope of uniting the South and the North, for he was the only Southern senator to support the Union. Curiously Booth had visited Johnson's hotel the afternoon of the assassination where he sent a note to the Vice President, "Don't wish to disturb you, Are you at home? J. Wilkes Booth." On finding Johnson gone he had the note put in Johnson's box. Atzerodt who had a room there was supposed to have been assigned to kill Johnson. But although both men were at the hotel at the appointed time, no apparent attempt was ever made.

Whether Booth did this to implicate Johnson or Johnson was in communication with the Secret Service of the South is not known. But Johnson was Southern born—pro the right to have slaves but a firm supporter of the Union, and the end result of the assassination made Johnson, a Southerner, President.

But what of Dr. Stone? What had his role been during the Civil War? Surely Mary Stone would never have known Booth, Herold, and John Surratt except through her father. Dr. Stone's nephew, Frederick Stone, was Counsel to David Herold, another nephew, Thomas Stone, had testified on behalf on the St. Albans' Raiders, and Booth, Herold, and Surratt appear in his daughter's album. The children's teacher, Emily Colton, was a cousin of two Sanders involved in the spy trail and the St. Albans' Raid, a Saunders, publisher of a "Bible View of Slavery," and Coltons in St. Albans and Georgia, Vermont. What of the strange coincidence of the J.H. Surratt handkerchief in the St. Albans' train station? It is impossible to think Dr. Stone had no role.

Across the Patuxent and below Benedict at Battle Creek, Union forces had established a military camp where an arsenal was built and which was used for the confinement of Confederate prisoners as well, called Prison Point. Across the creek and under the noses of Union troops at Brooke Place Manor, boats would leave in the dark of the night loaded with medical supplies for the Confederacy.

Naval engagements between Union blockaders and Southern blockade runners were not infrequent.

John Wilkes Booth's sister, Asia, wrote a book after the assassination published years later by a granddaughter in which she had asserted that all through the war Booth had smuggled medical supplies to the South—particularly desperately needed quinine water. I believe this was Dr. Stone's connection with Booth and probably how Dr. Mudd also knew Booth. Dr. Stone must have helped with smuggling medical supplies to the South.

And so ended the tragedy for the main players; a poor President who inherited the problems that were to bring a four year nightmare to a nation through no fault of his own; his misunderstood and unkindly thought of wife who may have inadvertantly brought about the death of her own husband; and three people hanged for what they considered to be patriotism—three who considered their actions to be an act of war, and one, Mrs. Surratt, who probably had nothing to do with the plot.

But the tragedy continued for the rest of the South. The blacks who were now free became the main sufferers. There was nowhere to go, there were no jobs, and worst of all there was no longer any one to have responsibility for their illnesses or their well-being, for welfare was non-existent in those days.

In families with a small number of slaves where they were part of the family relationship, there appears to have been little difference in their lives and so it was with Dr. Stone whose slaves stayed on as part of the family. In freedom the responsibility for their own welfare was sometimes an insurmountable burden for those on larger plantations.

On large plantations where planting was the mainstay of life it was disasterous for both the whites and the blacks. The blacks who were free refused to work, but with nowhere to go, the whites could not be so cruel as to send them away and so it was with Susan Somervell's parents at "Greenwood" with more than 100 slaves. The plantations deteriorated and it became tacky to show any sign of prosperity for to be prosperous became synomous with collaboration with the enemy. Til this day, genteel poverty is a hallmark of breeding in the South.

One of Dr. Stone's nephews, Thomas Stone, had testified for the St. Albans' Raiders in Canada. Another newphew, Frederick Stone, was counsel to David Herold. Frederick Stone became a judge in Charles County and later a U.S. Congressman. His tombstone at LaPlata says, "A Christian, a loving husband and father."

It is certain the people of Southern Maryland were not sorry that Lincoln was dead, that in some strange way on the heels of surrender the ultimate victory was theirs. Mary Stone Colton was not alone in honoring Booth with the first place in her photograph album.

Governor Oden Bowie, elected in 1869, named his son George Washington Booth Bowie, and one elderly

Virginia woman has even today three pictures hidden on the back of her closet door, one of Robert E. Lee, one of Jefferson Davis and one of John Wilkes Booth. She calls them the three greatest men who ever lived.

A young man, whose wife comes from Virginia, told me with some amusement that his wife had not known until she went to college that the South had lost the war. She had always been told that General Lee had agreed to a "Truce."

But a handful of sad but wise men in Southern Maryland who had fought for the Confederacy told their grandsons, the South never knew it, but Lincoln was the best friend they had ever had.

MARY STONE AND WALTER COLTON

The photograph of Mary Stone was taken from her sister's photograph album. The photograph of Walter Colton from Mary Stone's album was taken at least five years before their marriage.

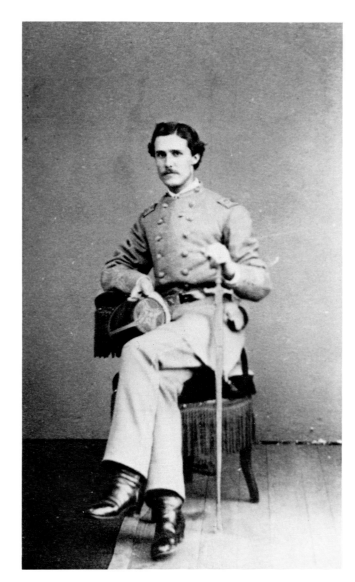

CHAPTER VIII   THE LAST HUNDRED YEARS

In 1870 Mary Stone married Walter Colton, brother of Aunt "Nina" Colton. Walter went to Texas where he had a role in building the railroad in the Texas panhandle. There near the Oklahoma border he founded a town which he called "Stratford," probably first of all because he honored the birthplace of Robert E. Lee, but also perhaps because the Lees of "Stratford" were his cousins and for the very brief period of 10 years "Stratford Hall" had belonged to his wife's bachelor cousin William Somerville.

The same year Mary Stone was married, Susan Somervell's brother, John Howe Somervell, applied to London to claim heir to the 20th Barony of Cambusnethan, through the succession of his father, Thomas Truman Somervell. The following is an obituary account from the "Illustrated London News" in September of 1870. "The Right Honorable Aubrey John Somerville nineteenth Lord Somerville . . . at his seat Somerville, Aston near Evesham.

". . . Thomas T. Somerville is the legitimate heir to this title.

"He asserted his claim to it, but there was no property attached to it . . . and the expenses of prosecuting were so great, that he was compelled to abandon it."

Thomas T. Somerville was Susan Somervell's father. Actually the claim was made through her brother John Howe, her father having died. The American inheritance passed to her father in 1825 at the death of William C. Somerville buried at Lafayette's estate, he being the last male descendent of John's line.

Oddly enough, during the life-time of William C. Somerville, another great-grandson of James Somervell, the Scottish prisoner, back in Scotland claimed the Marquisate de Somerville, the seat of which is near Evreux in France. His claim was denied but what is so interesting about this is that the lineage of his claim dated back to 1066 when the first de Somerville invaded England with William the Conqueror more than 700 years before.

Also, in 1870, a Colton cousin, Richard Colton, purchased part of the first Maryland land grant, St. Clement's Manor where he built a resort hotel. Curiously, it is opposite Stratford Hall on the Potomac. The land is still known as Colton Point.

Before the last decade of the 19th Century, "Auntie" went to the beautiful 18th Century "Tudor Hall" perched over Breton Bay near the mouth of the Potomac. Hers was a sad mission of a condolence call to the Key family. "Tudor Hall" had been purchased in the latter part of the 18th Century by Phillip Key, uncle of Francis Scott Key. In the kitchen was a forlorn little four year old girl who had just lost her mother. The child's distressed father came into the kitchen bewildered as to how he could care for this motherless little thing and "Auntie" who loved little girls asked to take her home for a visit and a time of love and attention. This is how Cora Key came to "Sunnyside" for she never went back.

It was a common practice for neighbors and relatives to take each other's children in time of need but this seems to apply almost exclusively to girls for boys were considered to be a problem and an expense.

Sometimes guardians appropriated the inheritance of their wards before there was an orphan's court. Such was the case of a little girl in the mid-18th Century. At sixteen she had married the son of her guardian. The young couple charged his father with stealing the bride's slaves and property. The Lord Proprietor appointed three judges to seek facts and determine the truth. The three men, one of whom was

James, the second, Somervell, were given a list of questions—was she given a silk bonnet according to her station in life or was she forced to wear a cotton one? Did she have a silk coat and did she have her own horse and saddle?

The findings were that the groom's mother had been kind and loving and had made no difference between the bride and her own children, but that the father had indeed taken the young girl's property for his own. The father was ordered to pay the young couple a large amount of tobacco.

Mary Stone Colton died while her two daughters were little girls. In Walter Colton's will he wrote, "since I have no home of my own I direct that I be buried beside my wife at Woodville." And so at St. Mary's Chapel at the corner of "Sunnyside" he is buried with his wife beside Dr. Stone, and his wife, Susan Somervell, and with his daughter Anna, and his granddaughter, Anna Lee.

Anna's daughter was to marry a naval officer who fought in World War I and World War II. Her grandson was to fight as a Marine, leading the detachment to clear the way for the raising of the flag on Mt. Surabachi at Iwo Jimo and later he was to fight at Vietnam. Both her great-grandsons fought at Vietnam. Somewhere Dr. Stone may be proud that surely every generation of his ancestors and of his descendents fought for their country in almost every, if not every war, in victory and defeat but always proudly.

When I sadly put my house up for sale a young man came several times with such obvious appreciation of a house so full of history—a house that one could feel in every room that it had been loved, that I was happy when he purchased it. But it was months after he had bought it that I was chatting about the new owner with a dear village friend. Telling her that his first name was Covington she was quite surprised and asked if he were any relation to the Covingtons of "Covington Farm" a few miles up the road and on the Patuxent River. Not far from the river we found a tombstone—a slab six feet long and four inches thick bearing the name Levin Covington and the date of his death 1745. His wife Margery Hollyday was the sister of an ancestor of mine. We think "Covey" came back to Woodville like a homing pigeon.

ST. MARY'S CHAPEL
Aquasco, Maryland

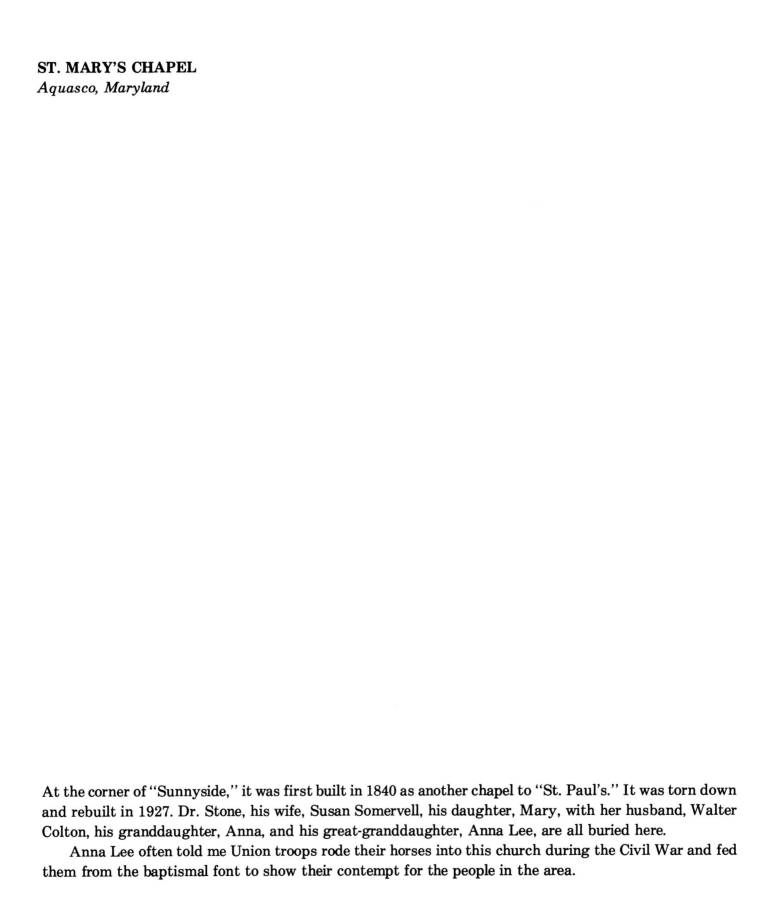

At the corner of "Sunnyside," it was first built in 1840 as another chapel to "St. Paul's." It was torn down and rebuilt in 1927. Dr. Stone, his wife, Susan Somervell, his daughter, Mary, with her husband, Walter Colton, his granddaughter, Anna, and his great-granddaughter, Anna Lee, are all buried here.

Anna Lee often told me Union troops rode their horses into this church during the Civil War and fed them from the baptismal font to show their contempt for the people in the area.

B. Taussig '81

AFTERWORD

Many of the items in the house have been given to Historic Annapolis and other museums.

Among items of interest were an 18th Century musket, an early Colt pistol, a mid-19th Century microscope from France, hand woven counterpanes in lovely patterns, baskets made by slaves, a doll house made by slaves, 18th Century furniture, and old prints. In the winter kitchen I found four sections of I knew not what, but when they were put together formed a horn made of copper and handsomely scrolled about four feet long. At one end was a loop. This turned out to be an old 18th Century coach horn which was hung by the fireplace of a tavern. It was used to let surrounding neighbors know when the coach had arrived.

Another curious item was an 18th Century traveling cup (as a child I was sure this was the "Holy Grail") for travelers in the 18th Century carried their own eating utensils.

Visiting was the major form of entertainment and several trundle beds were given to the Historical Society. One older relative told me that cousins would arrive and stay for months without notice since there were no telephones. Tournaments, parties, and visiting for young people began with the arrival of the first jonquil. The tournament, a modification of the ancient Norman sport, was a social event carried from generation to generation and is continued until today. Jousting is still the official sport of Maryland.

Some thousand books would have been quite valuable if they had not been damaged by mice, but it was some indication of how the children were educated. Books that included Latin and Greek and role-model stories for young ladies indicated that in the early years, although the children were taught at home, the educational process was treated seriously. Later the young girls were sent to a young ladies school run either by relatives or close friends. The young boys were sent to Charlotte Hall and later to St. Johns College, both military schools. Each child in the family had his or her own desk and school was held in a room over the slave quarters behind the house.

The ice house, a twenty foot hole in the ground with a roof was filled in January from the creek below and would last through the summer.

The winter kitchen had been converted to storage revealing that every member of the family had his own chest of personal treasures in addition to a small box. Mary Stone's trunk, made of wood and covered with canvas for protection, told of a strong lack of privacy when visiting at home, for between the canvas and the trunk I found love letters from her young husband hidden from the prying eyes of her unmarried sisters.

A box of arrowheads along with old tools and kitchen utensils were given to a small state museum at Clinton. Professional examination of one arrowhead proved it to come from a county in upstate New York where only a rare rock exists. This would indicate that the prosperous Southern Maryland Indians were raided from as far away as northern New York.

Given to a museum were four deguerrotypes found in Dr. Stone's treasure box, one of Jefferson Davis, one of Mrs. Davis, one of Robert E. Lee and one of General Beauregard. They were made by a New York company on Nassau Street in New York, who were apparently itinerent photographers during the Civil War.

Also given to a museum were the large and rare etching of Robert E. Lee, a small etching of Stonewall Jackson, a colored picture of General Lee's generals, and a photograph of Robert E. Lee on "Traveler," his horse. These items had been purchased by my grandfather in New York from Mary Lee, daughter of the great general, who was forced to sell her father's memorabilia finding herself destitute.

Several books by Sir Walter Scott found in the house made me wonder if the Scotts who owned an adjoining farm in the early 19th Century were related to that famous man, for Woodville abounds with Scottish families with noble ancestors.

BIBLIOGRAPHY

Printed Sources

Much of factual sources came from the Hall of Records in Annapolis—the ship's manifest of the "Godspeed," papers of the Provincial Territories, wills and land records. Other sources were county historical societies, Calvert County, St. Mary's County, Charles County, and county libraries.

"A History of Calvert County, Maryland" by Charles Stein. An excellent history and genealogical book.

"Yesterday In Old St. Mary's County" by Robert Pogue. A very good history of Maryland's first settled county and her role in the Revolution, the War of 1812, and the Civil War.

"History of Charles County, Maryland," Klapthor/Brown.

"Across The Years in Prince George's County" by Effie Gwyn Bowie, A remarkable genealogical book.

"Tales of a Grandfather" by Sir Walter Scott. A delightful history of Scotland.

"A Concise History of Scotland" by Sir Fitzroy Maclean.

Maryland marriages, 1634-1777.

"The Tiernan and Related Families."

"Daredevils of the Confederate Army" by Oscar A. Kinchen.

"The St. Albans' Raid" by Franklin-Lamoille Bank, St. Albans, Vermont.

"Memories of the Somervilles" by James Somerville, 11th Lord Somerville of Scotland edited in 1815 by Sir Walter Scott.

"The Man Who Killed Lincoln" by Philip Van Doren Stern. Embellished as a novel it is still a very good account of the assassination and Booth's ten days as a fugitive.

"The Stones of Poynton Manor" by Arthur Neumann, a genealogy of the Stone family.

"The Life of John Henry Hopkins" by one of his sons.

"The Hollyday Family" by James Bordley, Jr., M.D.